AF208020

THE ART
OF THE
SOLOPERFORMER

THE ART
OF THE
SOLOPERFORMER
*A Field Guide
to Stage and Podium*

STEVE RAPSON

SoloPerformer.com

Copyright © 2000 by Steve Rapson
All rights reserved

Published by:
The American Success Institute
5 North Main Street, Natick, MA 01760
www.success.org

Original illustrations by John Forcucci

The New Yorker cartoons © CartoonBank.com.

Printed in the United States of America
First Printing: August, 2000

Rapson, Steve.
    The Art of the SoloPerformer:
    A Field Guide to Stage and Podium/Steve Rapson.
ISBN 1-884864-14-7

To Rosemary,
Who makes all things possible

Contents

MATERIAL 71

PERFORMANCE 83

PUBLIC SPEAKING 121

Preface

If it were easy, everyone could do it. To stand alone in front of a group to speak or sing is not easy. There is a good chance, however, that you will do it. The allure of performing, or the necessity of making a speech, puts everybody on stage occasionally. Often we are thrust up there with few survival tools.

Comedian George Carlin, compares stage failure to death:

"I died."

"It was death out there."

"I bombed."

If you succeed, the violent imagery works in reverse.

"I killed 'em."

"I knocked 'em dead with my punch line."

Every performer knows the emotional rip tide of stage success and failure. Nothing feels as good as when you win the audience, or as bad as when you lose them.

When you stand alone on stage, the path to success is the same no matter what you do there: speak, sing, preach, or teach. My experience as a television producer, speaker, and entertainer prompted this revelation, which now seems like common sense. All performers have one goal: to connect with their audience.

When I started this book, I tried to focus on either entertaining or speaking. However, I could not separate the two. Although I include a separate section on each, they are a pair, and the rules of each overlap enough to make them a single art.

Here are the stage survival tools you need to perform at your best, to kill, and to not die.

Introduction

This book is about how to do your best as a soloperformer, and how to connect with an audience. Why is it so easy one night and impossible the next, even with great material? What can you do to improve and have more great nights?

Our most relentless critic is within. Mine works for free and loves overtime. I was not going to release my first CD, *Christmas Guitar*, because I wanted to keep re-recording. My friend, Mary Gauthier, said, "It's fine. Stop waiting to be perfect; it's a long wait." It is hard to see when we have done our best.

We do our best when we ebb and flow with the forces that move us. Nowhere is this truer than on the stage and podium. Trying too hard is easy to spot. Notwithstanding the first line of Dr. Scott Peck's famous book *The Road Less Traveled*—'Life is difficult'—the path of least resistance seems to be the right one.

I attend poetry readings, speeches and musical open mikes of all kinds. I have met natural performers who zoom through the ranks to command large audiences and healthy sales of books, CDs and T-shirts. For others, every gain was a painful struggle. Each night, at small venues around Boston, hundreds of performers stand to deliver their songs, poems and stories. We are with each other, but alone in a private search for the way to connect with our audience. There are many doors to walk through, and we grow with each one.

Personal growth is difficult. Assisting others in *their* personal growth is easier. It is easier to give advice than take it. Easier to give criticism than hear it, easier to talk about action than to act. Growth and action create change. Change is the unknown. The unknown is the root of all fear. Fear is the great immobilizer. I wrote this book to illuminate the unknowns of performing. Nevertheless, it is still easier to write about the unknown than it is to know it.

Personal growth or personal disaster is always triggered by change. After twenty-five years of being Steve Rapson of The Gillette Company,

I was set adrift. With no anchor to keep me grounded, I left my wife and college-aged children in Boston and went to Phoenix, Arizona. I lived in a cinder block cubicle at the downtown YMCA for a few days. I heard shouts in the halls from other men with no place to go but here. I thought of my father, also a lost soul, who had died a month before in a similar place. I had no job, no friends, no family, no money, and no prospects. The next morning I sat in the desert sun with the following dialogue in my thoughts:

"What's the problem?"

"I'm lost. I don't know what to do."

"What do you want to do?"

"I don't know. That's the problem."

"Given total discretion what would you spend your time doing?"

"Play guitar."

"What else?"

"Write."

"One more?"

"Read."

"You have identified three things you would do given total freedom of action. It appears you have nothing else pressing now. Start doing one of them."

I wrote. After a while I played my guitar. Later, I finished my book.

Since then I have made my living with guitar and pen. I have not earned money by reading, keeping it purely recreational. I came home and my family let me in. I have made many new friends. Occasionally they leave 'to make room for others to enter,' said one who later left. It is a good thought, and I am blessed with a plentitude of others. Rational thinking helped.

If you are an artist, you may believe, as I do, that rationality diminishes creativity. Although rigor and systematic work are required to create, the moment of creation is usually serendipitous and unexpected, arriving fully formed while we are otherwise engaged. Charles Darwin, Richard Feynman, and Mozart attest this to. My creative side wants to avoid the rational truths that come unbidden whenever I think about how to be a successful performer.

Success in the arts is different from business success. The respect of one's peers helps with feeling successful, if not in looking successful. When another guitar player admires my work, that feels like success to me. My secret weapon for financial success in music is a wife who works. Thanks to my wife, Rosemary. I told this gag to my Arabic hosts on a visit to Rabat, Morocco. They frowned and said, via my interpreter:

"We believe a man who depends on his wife for money loses respect."

"Ah, yes... well," I said. "It's a joke... *ha-ha*. Very funny in America... you know, like Woody Allen says, *No wife of mine will ever work, I'm afraid to be home alone.*" More blank stares. Some material won't travel.

Through years of coaching others, I have learned how to coach myself. All self-help books are written first to the self. Fear, doubt and insecurity wear masks of arrogance and narcissism, masks of bluster and blunder, of timidity and hesitation. Removing one's masks is the first step to connecting with your audience.

PHILOSOPHY

1
What Do Good Performers Have In Common?

They are entertaining. As in, "Entertain this idea for a moment." When you are entertaining, you send a stream of words, sounds, and images that the audience allows in. They decide every few minutes, seconds even, whether they will continue to pay attention to you, or whether to think of something else, look somewhere else, and go somewhere else.

I first grappled with this at the Gillette Company, where I filmed corporate executives perched on the edge of their desks, hiding behind them, or, most frighteningly, walking around them. Frightening, because I saw how easy it was for a competent person to appear incompetent in an artificial situation. Just being normal was the problem, never mind being engaging and entertaining; few were able to do it.

I was personally required to be entertaining with my rock band. I noticed my rendition of *Blue Suede Shoes* had much in common with *The President's Message to Sales and Marketing*. For example, presidents are expected to look presidential, and rock singers, too, must look the part they play. Further, speakers and singers need to be committed to their material. I filmed executives who were not committed to his or her words, and the audience yawned though many a boring corporate video. Similarly, as my commitment to *Blue Suede Shoes* diminished, we became another boring wedding band, got less gigs, and eventually stopped playing.

Good performers never lose that element of excitement and breathless anticipation, no matter how practiced or experienced they may be. Breathless anticipation is harnessed stage fright. The harness is preparation and commitment. When you are committed to your act, you will practice far more than what most would call normal. Preparation and commitment make you entertaining.

2
Are Performers Born or Can I Learn the Skills?

There are natural performers, as well as people whom we say have charisma. Charisma is an internal light natural to some. They may be stars, con artists, and even sociopaths, who are often charismatic. You do not need charisma to be successful. Performance skills can be learned by anyone with the desire. Your desire must be inversely proportional to your ability: the harder it is for you the more you have to want it, and work for it.

Most performers learn by osmosis. It is natural and imitative. One can earn a degree in performance art and read books like this one. Politicians and comedians have no formal system for learning the skills of their calling. The two have a deep commonality that escapes analysis and method.

Corporate speakers are often boring and ineffective, usually due to a large ego and small preparation. I filmed a *Marketing Address to Factory Workers* starring a VP whose script had been written for him by a subordinate. As the crew made final adjustments, he walked in.

"We're going to make you a star." I said to put him at ease.

"I already am a star," he said.

His talking head was the worst I produced. He was obviously not committed as he spoke in a frozen-faced monotone. His poor preparation kept him glued to the teleprompter like a zombie on a mission. He was not afraid, only arrogant. Arrogance is the opposite of charisma.

Charismatic performers have the ability to focus on others. They suppress their own egos for a time to make others feel important and listened to. You can learn to do this and be charismatic yourself.

There are two kinds of performers. The good performer enters with, *"Here I am!"* The charismatic performer enters with, *"There you are!"*

© 2000 The New Yorker Collection from cartoonbank.com. All Rights Reserved

"But, seriously..."

3
What Skills Can A Performer Develop?

Performance skills are not what you say, but how you say it. They are the ribbons and bows that dress up your ideas. All performers and speakers use them, teachers, for example, or the Rolling Stones, the President in the Oval Office, and the doctor lecturing in the surgical theater.

First, however, you must have good material. Don White[1] says learning performance skills before you have something good to perform, is like putting a pig in a prom dress: *Nice dress, too bad it's wrapped around a pig.*

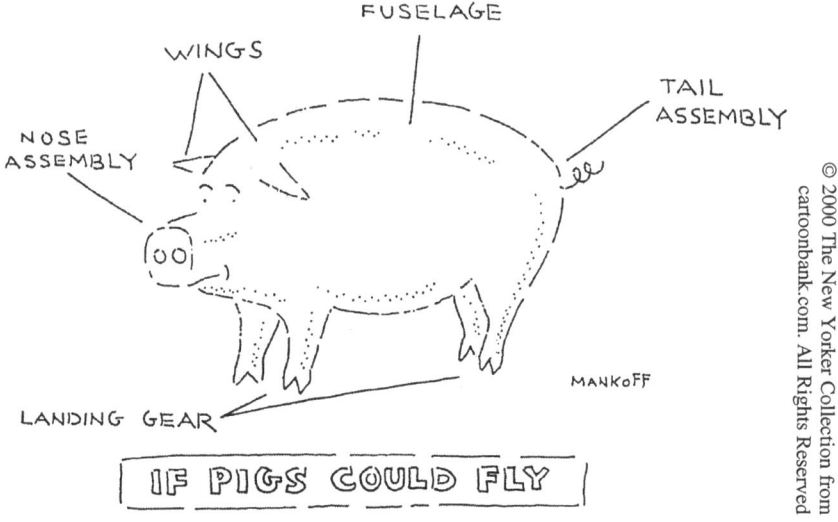

© 2000 The New Yorker Collection from cartoonbank.com. All Rights Reserved

The prom dress—performance technique—includes *Stage Presence*: How you carry yourself, who you look at, your facial expressions.

Body Language: How you move, what you do with your hands.

Timing: Your pace, how you command the silence.

---

[1] Don White is a songwriter and performer from Lynn, Massachusetts. His act was developed over many years in the music business trenches. We have had many conversations on the art of the stage.

How to hold and speak into a microphone. How to speak without a microphone. How to handle a heckler or a non-responsive audience. How to relax with deep breathing. How to bow. How to enter and exit the stage. Advanced skills include internal work on humility and emotional accessibility.

Finally, the most difficult to master: learning to be yourself. Media advisor-to-presidents, Roger Ailes, calls this *being you at your best*. These all can be learned. If you already have these skills, they can be improved after you have your material ready for an audience.

4
Can Performance Skills Help Me In Other Areas Of My Life?

Effective performers cut to the essentials of a song or story. If you develop the habit for your stage work, you will know how to do it in normal conversation. You become sensitive to cliched phrases and verbal crutches. Some favorites are:

OK?...
Really...
a lot of...
very..., or the more impactful, *very, very...*
You know what I mean?... You know what I'm sayin'?...
But, ahh...
umm...
err...

These are called speaker noises. We all make them, but they can be controlled and eventually eliminated.

You learn how to get to the point: what to say, what to leave out. Buddhist monk and essayist Yoshida Kenko (1283-1350) said, "...leaving something incomplete makes it interesting, and gives one the feeling that there is room for growth."

If you have learned to overcome stage fright, then you have the tools to stay calm and centered in other stressful situations. If you have learned to be open, friendly and welcoming to an audience, you might be more like that socially.

5
Isn't Stage Performing Like Acting?

An actor's mission is to portray a character truthfully. A soloperformer's mission is to portray him or her self truthfully.

Acting requires skill not necessary for speaking and singing. That skill is to portray emotions you are not feeling. Method acting, on the other hand, requires you to find the feeling from your life and let it infuse your being so that you are not "cold" when acting the part.

There are adherents to each school. In either case, it takes skill that some say, Michael Redgrave for one, it is not possible to teach. For non-actors it is only necessary that you be who you are. No acting required.

6
Who Are Some Great Soloperformers?

The standard for singer /songwriters is blues master Robert Johnson, as evidenced by his hotel room recordings. Jazz singer Billie Holiday is in this category, too. Judy Garland and daughter Liza Minelli had, and have, the power to move their audience. John Gorka, wrote *Heart Upon Demand,* a song about Judy's emotional accessibility that endeared her even more than her vocal talents. Don White, whose thoughts and experience I liberally quote, is known for his emotionally charged shows that alternately move the audience to laughter and tears.

In the speaking arena, the great Greek orator Pericles admired the greater Demosthenes saying, "When Pericles speaks, the people say, 'How well he speaks'. But when Demosthenes speaks the people say, 'Let us march'. "

People paid dearly and stood in long lines for an evening of stories written and told by Mark Twain (1835-1910). Politician, William Jennings Bryan (1860-1925) could hold an audience for three hours while he spoke on issues of the day.

Today, Garrison Keillor of PBS's *A Prairie Home Companion* is a master of the radio monologue. Similarly, Spaulding Gray sits at a desk and just talks. His talks have become Broadway shows and movies like *Swimming to Cambodia*. Rosemary and I recently saw Mr. Gray's latest show, *Morning, Noon, and Night*.

"What is the show about?" Rosemary asked.

"He sits at a desk on an empty stage and talks," I said.

"What does he talk about?"

"His life, usually."

"It sounds boring."

The theater was sold out. Spaulding Gray was riveting, with brilliant writing and an engaging presentation. Rosemary loved it. I took notes.

Both Gray and Keillor speak in an impromptu style, as if their words were spontaneously occurring to them. Preachers, like Martin Luther King, Jr., and his protégé, Rev. Jesse Jackson, speak in stentorious tones with a message less vulnerable to style. Politicians will adopt a similar oratorical style to bolster their airy words.

When content is weak, a speaker may use style and high position for cover. The weaker the material, the more puffed up the package. Conversely, the stronger the material the plainer the wrapper can be. For example, "Confession is good for the soul," is a strong statement. What is the most effective way to say it? Shouted wild-eyed, feverishly, or in a matter-of-fact manner? What every speaker wants is to move the people with the ideas and biblical sonority of a man like Dr. King, one of the great orators of the 20th Century.

Loretta LaRoche, www.stressed.com, appears on Public Television during fund raising. She is a fine speaker with excellent material, a succinct message, and a humorous, natural style.

Among comics and comic actors: Charlie Chaplin, Jackie Gleason, and Richard Pryor are legends of the art whose work transcends time and their own personal foibles.

For teachers, look into your own memory banks. A teacher is burned into your mind because of the impression he or she made on you.

If you can recall what made him or her memorable, you will have a piece of the puzzle to what makes a great soloperformer.

7
What Makes A Soloperformer Effective?

Did we feel something? Effective performers evoke strong emotions in us. We laugh. We cry. We think. While evoking emotion, they are always in control. The biggest laughs come when the performer is not laughing, but ranting. The most heartfelt emotions sneak up on us, as a performer reveals a truth that suddenly connects to our own lives. He enters our consciousness through the filter of our own experience. Because of what we let in, we see ourselves differently and have a personal revelation. We are moved to laughter or tears.

Beginners think the purpose of their material is to shed light on themselves, to lift their inner selves into view. A pro knows their purpose is to shed light on the material, to lift the idea, and connect the audience to a deeper part of themselves. Singer/songwriter Mary Gauthier's essay says this well.

The Stage, The Work, The Truth
An Open Letter To Myself
by
Mary Gauthier[2]

When I take the stage I must be humble. Humility is the only worthy response to the trust the audience will put in me. True humility makes me successful; false humility makes me look foolish. I will stand tall and look the audience in the eyes, one by one, and let them know I am comfortable, confident, and humble.

If ambition and the hunger for applause have driven me to the stage, then I should not disgrace myself by having nothing to

[2] Mary Gauthier sold her successful restaurant, Boston's *Dixie Kitchen,* to pursue her dream of song writing and performing. She has become widely known for well-crafted songs. Her latest CD, *Drag Queens in Limousines*, was one of the hottest of 1999.

say. It is my job to articulate what everybody already knows but does not say. I must do this so that people will respond to me as they would a friend. I must speak and sing clearly. My words must ring true. The second that I waver from the truth they will know it.

I cannot afford to oversell my music. It speaks for itself. I must pull my stories from deep inside myself, then go deeper still. This is where the truth is. I must not put on airs or try to impress. If I give the people what is real, this will impress without effort: this will impress most of all. I must never pretend to be the star looking down on my audience. This is repulsive; people will turn on me.

I am not smarter than my audience. I am not more beautiful. I am a mirror, reflecting to the people what is already theirs. If people laugh or cry, we do so together. This will not happen if I am feeling discomfort brought on by raging ego.

I cannot have their attention for free. I must give them something. What must I give them? What do people—what do I—really need? We need to get closer to the essence of ourselves. The artist can help the people do this. The artist is a risk taker who must expose his or her self and thereby reveal to the audience their own selves; and, in this public act, form a community. People hunger for community and authenticity. If they are given ego instead of honesty, they will be put off.

I must not affect my behavior or act out of false emotion. This will leave the audience staring at my ambition. Ambition is close to my ego. It must be tempered with humility, or the people will not like what they see. I believe that any talent I posses has been given to me by my Creator, and through discipline, humility and truth, I can shine the light back on my Higher Power. I have no power to create without the help of my Creator. I must take no credit for it. I do not deserve this credit, and my ego will never be satisfied by it anyway. Give the glory to the Creator of all that is.

I write and sing my truth and that makes me brave, but I must not confuse courage with blessings. Bravado is false; it does not ring true.

I am not a commercial. I should not be self serving. The people endure too many commercials. My job is to seek the truth and show it. Nothing is more essential. A beautiful singing voice is loved, but if it sings platitudes it will never matter. Beautiful costumes and a gorgeous body cannot hide the ugliness of vanity and conceit. Youthfulness is no substitute for content. Not in the long run. I need not fear these things.

I should not waste my time chasing the light. The light will come to me if I am honest, because the light follows truth. If I follow truth, the light will follow me. I know this, but I forget it. Show up for my truth, sing it wherever they will let me, and be patient.

I should not pretend to know what I do not yet know, nor pretend to comprehend that which I do not yet understand. This is not honest and it will block me from finding the truth. The people will know that I am faking it and they will distance themselves from me. I cannot look good all of the time, I should not be afraid of my humanity. My mistakes connect me with people as well, because the audience appreciates vulnerability. People will appreciate my sadness if I am sad, my happiness if I am happy, my anger if I am mad. Fake an emotion and they will know it. I am not an actor. I am a reporter, reporting the truth. Many truths are hard for me to look at. But if I see them in me, and tell them, the people will respond. Although I am afraid to expose myself to them, I must do this nightly.

This is my job; this is the job of every artist. I should be assertive, be confident, be humble, be honest and true. If I am blessed and touched with grace, and if I am willing to go through the pain of this, I will be called an artist, and I will be whole.

8
What Are The Elements Of A Good Act?

Be prepared. Be interesting. Be yourself.

Be Prepared. You are prepared when you have a story to tell, and practice the telling until it is airtight. Few in the lower echelons do it. Today, for example, I heard a group of musicians interviewed on local college radio. They had nothing of interest to say beyond, "Yeah, well, we've known each other a bunch of years, and, yeah, well ya' know, it's been great." They attempted spontaneous wit about their upcoming concert, "Be there, or be… somewhere else." They went on for endless minutes about getting old. They laughed nervously at their own quips which were not funny. They were woefully unprepared to tell "Our story so far…" On the other hand, their music was excellent. If you have nothing to say, say nothing. Do what you have prepared to do. Be spontaneous only after you have planned it thoroughly.

In 1968, Andy Warhol said, "In the future, everybody on earth will be famous for fifteen minutes." You will get more time if you are ready.[3] *Be Interesting.* Condense the details of your life. Tell what you have seen and what you have learned. Tell your most embarrassing moment, and other stories. You are interesting when you tell secrets. Gossip is interesting. We hate ourselves for liking it. We like it nonetheless. Make the gossip about yourself, and they will like you. Filter your reading and research through your experience. Report your results. It is gossip no more, but revelation. You are interesting when you surprise them as well as fulfill their expectations. A hit song is 80% predictable and 20% surprise.

You are interesting when you do not oversell. As your story or song unfolds, you discover along with the audience. Robert Frost said, "No tears in the writer, no tears in the reader. No surprise for the writer, no surprise for the reader." Write it, edit it, rehearse it, and try it out.

Be yourself. I hoped to write about performing without reference to this overworked maxim. "Oh, just be yourself!" is the axiom offered by your friends and family. Little do they know it is the tallest of orders, because it is hard to be natural in unnatural circumstances. You are natural when do not try too hard. If you have not had some practice at this, you will not be able to do it.

The complete you is complex. You are serious and methodical, you are spontaneous and light-hearted; you are earnest, empathetic, ironic, tongue-in-cheek, playful, sincere, angry, sad, and happy. You must let all of you show while, above all, you are being interesting. Interesting takes preparation and practice. This paradox confounds new performers: *How can I be spontaneous if I have to do the same thing every time?*

Consider jazz musicians, who are known as improvisers. Musical improvising is spontaneous composition. It is the removing and surpassing of musical boundaries, and is the highest form of the art.

However, before a jazz player can improvise, he must learn the melody, the rhythm, and the related chords and scales. Everything must be practiced as written until it is automatic and can be played without thought or hesitation. Only then can he improvise. New notes are introduced; some are left out. Fast passages, slow passages, and

---

[3] British author, Martin Amis, in *Experience: A Memoir,* revised Warhol, observing that, today, everybody is famous all the time… in their own minds, because everybody has a book in him: an autobiography.

surprising harmonic twists which seem to magically resolve where they ought. Jazz musicians prepare to be spontaneous.

When you speak to or perform for an audience, you can improvise and be spontaneous, but only after you have written, learned, and practiced everything until you know it cold.

9
Why Is Video Important?

It is the performer's lie detector. There are two kinds of lies. The first is, *Man! I was great!* The second is, *God! I was awful.* We invoke God only in times of distress. A tape of your performance lets you see the truth. The truth lies somewhere between man and God.

There is nothing more revealing than a tape of your show, especially a few days afterwards. An objective eye will let you see what is good about your act, and what is not working. Keep the good and dump the bad. Be tough. This is how good acts are developed.

As a side benefit you will have a recording of those spontaneous moments where you do something unplanned but brilliant. These are the gems to collect and burnish into your act. They came spontaneously from you. They are you at your best. This is how to get material that kills. It is hard to re-create a bit that popped out of you spontaneously. Even with a recording you will have to rehearse it to get the timing right. The first time it was natural. Every other time, you are doing a bit. It is different.

WACT-TV in Ashland, Massachusetts produces a music program called *Unplugged.* My partner, Maureen Keiller, and I appeared recently. The playback was hard for me to watch. I was nervous. My hands were scratching at my head and face. I was squirming around, and I was too fat. On the positive side, our act and material were excellent. Our voice lessons showed results and we played off each other in a likable way.

I have since lost thirty pounds as a direct result of seeing, objectively, how it would be much better if I were not so fat. I have redoubled my discipline to control random body movements and to keep my hands away from my face when I feel nervous. The next step is to practice and prepare a little more, so I do not feel so nervous.

Be a pro. Record your act. Wait a few days. Watch and learn.

© 2000 The New Yorker Collection from cartoonbank.com. All Rights Reserved

10
What Is The Best Way
To Beat Disappointment?

Disappointment is unfulfilled expectation or unsatisfied cravings. If one neither expects nor craves, then disappointment is handily sidestepped. For example, if you parachuted out of an airplane with the objective of just landing anywhere safely, then a happy outcome is probable. Good things happen when your mind is open to all possibilities. A narrow definition of what will make you happy courts disappointment. This may sound indecisive if you believe focussed objectives are the way to success. However, I believe an attitude of acceptance is the way to mental toughness. It is being gig-tough.

Gig-tough performers are the ones most likely to connect with a crowd. This is because they have developed the ability to do their best in any situation. An audience detects how an artist feels from the subtlest clues. Being gig-tough means thinking less.

My *Christmas Guitar Tour* included nineteen gigs in twenty-one days: an open mike feature, The Tam, Borders Books, Passim, two radio interviews, restaurants, coffee shops, and living rooms. I hated the first several gigs. I thought the sound was bad and my playing was poor. The audience was indifferent. Nobody bought my CDs. I thought, *"What am I doing here?"* Halfway through the tour, things improved. I began to enjoy my playing. People sang along, and I sold some product.

Perhaps the secret was a good room, or a good crowd, or the planets in alignment. However, on the night it got better I was in the same room as the miserable week before. I wore the same clothes and played the same songs on the same guitar. The only variable was my thinking. After several gigs in a row, I became gig-tough and got immersed in the sound of the guitar; executing the parts I had carefully worked out. I was in the zone.

One Friday night at Strawberry Fair Restaurant I came out of the zone after an extended improvisation on *Moonlight In Vermont.* I played re-harmonized melody, dissonant chords and exotic scales. *"Hmmm, this is an interesting turn around..."*

People politely clapping. *Where...? What...?*

"Whoa! Forgot where I was," I said to the group grinning on my left. This is where I want to be every time I perform. I have a better time, and so does the audience.

Think less. Especially avoid thinking about how the gig is going while performing. It diminishes your ability to connect. You do not get in the zone, and are too aware of distractions in the room:

Geez, could those two talk any louder over there?

Is the sound technician intentionally trying to sabotage me?

This stage is too high; I can't connect.

This stage is too low; my space is being violated.

Oh, no! They're going to smoke right in front of me!

This kind of thinking weakens you. It is the opposite of being gig-tough. As you grow and develop true mental toughness, here are some ideas that may speed the process.

Be humble. Humility comes from outside ourselves. Find a source.

Be empty of expectations. Expectations come from our own thoughts. Think less.

Be gig-tough. Do a lot of gigs. Always be ready to work. When you have eight offers a week, then be picky.

The purpose is to develop an ability to personally connect with the audience via the music. Audience communication and connection is the goal of all performing.

Boston television reporter Gail Harris interviewed Bruce Marks, Director of the Boston Ballet. She asked him what he looks for in a dancer. He said, "Well, everybody who comes to the Boston Ballet is highly skilled. Technical perfection is a given at this level. I look for that spark of human connection: a dancer who takes in the audience with her eyes. Laura Young (Boston Ballet School principal dancer) can make eye contact with three hundred people at the same time. You can see it going forth from the stage out to the theater, and back from them to her. The great ones all make that personal connection."

Terry Gross interviewed poet/rocker Patti Smith on the NPR show Fresh Air. Terry asks,

"You started off reading your poetry in bars?"

"Yes," said Patti. "Normally they had bands, but on off nights, or as an opening act, I would get to do fifteen or twenty minutes. At first people would ignore me or even try to shout me off the stage. But I stayed up there and wouldn't be driven off; eventually I started to connect. The last few minutes they paid attention."

Expect nothing and you are prepared for everything. Be gig-tough, like Ms. Smith.

11
Are All Audiences The Same?

In general, yes. Individuals vary enormously. Groups of people behave in more predictable ways. For example, traffic patterns, people in cars, are so predictable that there are mathematical models for their behavior. As audience size increases language and cultural differences decrease. The language of music is universal. A song in minor keys denotes sadness and pathos. A tempo faster than a human heartbeat induces excitement.

In the era of silent movies, Charlie Chaplin was an international star. He was known intimately everywhere. Clowns and mimes can work in China or England without varying their act in the slightest. Of course, if your act is language-based then it is a little more complex. Words are not always required, however.

In the *Four Noble Truths*, a video series, the Dali Lama addressed a London audience primarily in Tibetan via his interpreter. His body language and personal charisma transcended the language barrier. He smiled and nodded to individual audience members in a most charming way. Words were not necessary for him to connect on a deep personal level with them.

At the Intercontinental Hotel in Madrid, I organized sales meetings for our Spanish distributors. I wanted my introductory speech to connect with them, but I spoke no Spanish. Christof, my interpreter, translated my three-minute talk, and then wrote it phonetically for me to practice. I spent the next two days learning it verbatim, with much coaching on pronunciation, pauses and the like. In the bathtub, in the cab, at dinner, I beat that Spanish speech to death. When it came time to deliver it I warned my audience that I did not really speak Spanish and was only able to address them briefly in their language. I then walked from behind the lectern, paused, and spoke Spanish.

Nineteen year old Christof—speaker of five other languages—had done such a good job with me that the assembled sales force refused to believe that I was not totally fluent in their native tongue. For the remainder of the meeting I moved among them, smiling and nodding to their rapid-fire, amiable chatter, only occasionally needing the translation help of Christof. There is nothing like a language barrier to boost one's listening skills!

Non-verbal communication is more immediate than words. A smile is universally recognized as welcome, friendship and relaxation. A nod of the head is affirmation. Shaking the head is negation. Arms spread wide means acceptance. Bowing indicates humility and gratitude. In fact, 80% of communication is visual.

Natural movements motivated by our feelings are different than conscious gestures designed to communicate a thought. Cultivate the right mental state and your body language will follow and speak clearly to all other humans. What this means to a performer is that once you have figured out your message and its method of conveyance, you can be reasonably sure it is going to work wherever you go.

12
What Should I Do For My Fans?

Give them what they want: your time, talent, and preparation, your enthusiasm, your hard work. Be like James Brown, the hardest working man in show business. Make them drag you away.

Be like Ruth Brown. Tell the truth. "You deal with the truth when you're singing the blues," she says, "you got to live'em a little to sing'em." Be like Les Brown, "If you fall down, make sure you land on your back, because if you can look up, you can get up."

Be like the late Leo Buscaglia. Love them. Listen to them. Performing is not about fame. It is about connecting with your fans. You do not need many to have a satisfying career. You do need to take good care of the ones you have.

Greg Abate is a bebop alto sax player. He is described in what press he gets as underrated and under appreciated, a virtuoso whose rewards are insufficient for his talent. There may be several reasons for this. I know only one of them.

Rosemary and I went to see Mr. Abate perform in Falmouth, Massachusetts. He was booked at the local community center in Woods Hole, an old New England building with big double doors and tall windows along the sides. It was a dark and woody place with creaking floors and good-sized stage. A woman took tickets just inside the front door. Another sold Greg Abate CDs from behind a table stacked high with his several titles. The hall could hold two hundred and fifty people. About twenty-five had come to see the show. We took our pick of front row seats as the musicians greeted friends in the audience. After forty-five minutes of virtuoso jazz and bebop, Mr. Abate said they would be back after a break. Rosemary sighed. She is not fond of *be,* or *bop,* nor the combination.

Break time is a break from playing, not a break from working to build your fan base. Especially at this level. A break is the time to step down from the bandstand to greet the few souls who are paying your wages. It is a time to shake hands, smile warmly and invite the loyalists to check out the new CD for sale and, while there, to snap up older titles not available in stores. Mr. Abate and company might have stood behind the table to autograph CDs and tell what musical adventures awaited in the second set.

However, what the band did was march wordlessly out of the hall, zip across the street, and park themselves at the local bar. Every man creates his own happiness, and happiness has its price. The price that day was lost opportunity to further their music. New fans were not made. Names for the mailing list were lost. A few hundred dollars in CDs were not sold. At how many performances have Mr. Abate and company done similarly? Could this account for his rewards being insufficient to his obvious talent?[4]

In the entertainment business it is a cliché that talent is sixth or seventh among the top ten things that make for a successful career. It is all in who you know, and who knows you. Sometimes we do all the right things to connect and still we are met with indifference and no sales. It is easy to be lovable when you are loved. Success in this business requires you do the right thing every time, even when the pain of rejection and apathy lingers from the night before.

Your fans are made one at a time. It is easier to keep the ones you have than to find and convert new ones. A warm body in a room to see you is 90% converted. Do not blow it by failing to walk the final yard to connect with your audience.

---

[4] Please do not think I am judging harshly the talented and likeable Mr. Abate. I have been in his shoes many times, and have done the same thing (the bar part, not the brilliant jazz part.) The highest joy of a gig is quite often the socializing with one's peers before, during, and after. We all want our cake; and we want to eat it, too.

13
How Do I Know If I Am Any Good?

You will never know for sure, no matter how you succeed. Good and Bad are Platonic absolutes. They are meaningless unless referenced to some standard. The marketplace is the final determinant for financial success. Critical acclaim is another. Fame and fortune are obvious standards for success. Nonetheless, dissatisfaction among the rich and famous is legendary.

During my twenty-five years in corporate America I learned that organizational standards are external, impersonal, and objective. They are artificial and often easy to achieve. Individual standards for success are internal, personal, and subjective; sometimes they are impossible to achieve. For example, one thing I always wanted was to have my father tell me I was a good guitar player. He never did.

I have friends who are CEO's and media stars. Objectively, from the outside, they appear to meet all standards for success. But I know there are times when they sit behind closed doors wondering when they will be revealed as the failures and incompetents they sometimes feel they are. This happens when we compare ourselves to spectacularly successful people. It is hard not to notice the extremes of success, because this is where the media looks for stories. Better that you make your role models those not so famous but highly successful people. If you are going to compare, you might as well find some people with whom you can compare favorably.

One way to measure your own success without comparing is to set realistic goals with small steps for achieving them. This way, you are successful everyday because you move closer to your goal with each little step. My daily goal is to stay focussed on the three things I want to do (playing guitar, reading, writing) and not do what I *wish* I would want to do. This is a collorary to Stuart Brand's admonition in the Whole Earth Catalog (1970): "It is important to distinguish between those tools you need from those tools you *wish* you needed."

Your realistic goal could be, "Sell A Million CDs." The realistic part is to divide the big goal, which is not likely to happen today, into small bites which *will* be done today. Miracles do occur, as do big breaks; and we may exceed our capacity to perform. However, you cannot put these happy events into your daily action plan. Every success story includes serendipitous events which we sometimes call miracles. Serendipity occurs when preparedness meets opportunity. Even when you have planned, prepared, and prayed for success, it often arrives from a different direction than you expected. It's a miracle.

Evaluations occur after the game has been played. While you are playing it is better to have fun. If you keep playing until your time is up, you will have had all the fun, while someone else gets the job of totaling the score.

Process is what we do, and outcome is what happens. The two are not so connected. G. B. Shaw's character, Menoza, in *Man and Superman* (1903) observed:

Sir, there are two tragedies in life. One is to lose your heart's desire. The other is to gain it. This quip is also attributed to Oscar Wilde.

Stay one step ahead of tragedy by thinking up new things for your heart to desire. Earl Nightingale said, "We are happiest when possessed by a good idea." Stay possessed, and the question of good or bad might never come up.

© 2000 The New Yorker Collection from cartoonbank.com. All Rights Reserved

14
When Is It Time To Give Up?

Even if you are making a decent living as a performer, if you are bored and unfulfilled with your daily activities, then it might be time to do something else. In 1974, after being booted out of other bands, I formed my own. As the leader, I would not fire myself. Fearlessly, I called everywhere for gigs. After dozens of, "No, go away." Club manager, Steve Campbell said, "I'm glad you called." It was the start of a fifteen-year run for one of Boston's most successful cover bands, The Music Company.

We rehearsed once a week. I handed out tapes so band members could get their parts down before rehearsal. I hustled for gigs, took voice lessons[5] auditioned singers and players, created promotional material, and produced demo tapes. Most weekends we had two or three gigs. In the beginning, I could not wait to hook up the trailer and be a rock star until Monday rolled around. I was possessed. Twelve years later, I thought, "Nuts! I have to do that gig tonight." I should have quit then. However, I dragged it out, working only for the money. Eventually, I quit music for five years. Then I returned as a solo acoustic guitarist. With no equipment to haul and no band members to coddle, I am possessed again.

If you are not happy with your performing maybe you need a rest. After the rest, if you do not have the overpowering urge to return, that is a clue to move on. On the other hand, if the source of your next meal is

---

[5] Babette Saltman was my first voice teacher. I had auditioned several of her students for the female lead in my band. I did not sing at the time, but wanted to try lessons. I asked her if I could study with her. Although she had a long waiting list, she said she would audition me. I had lent prestige to her studio, she said, by providing an opportunity for her students. She was an elderly, waifish woman with a commanding presence. At my audition, with no guitar to hide behind, her piano player accompanied me on *All I Have To Do Is Dream*. She sat scrunched up five feet away, chin in her hand, as I sweated and stumbled through it. Finally, she pronounced, "First of all, you're too fat. And I don't know what to do about your pitch problems." I smiled bravely. She continued, "You've got a decent tone, so maybe there's some hope." She took me on, and like all her students, I adored her.

in question, if the transmission just fell out of your car, if the hat was empty last night, but you still can't wait to do it again, keep on doing it, presuming no one else is depending on you for food, shelter, and all the rest.

Another strategy is to identify what is not to your liking. Maybe it is the road, or the smoky bars, or your geography. In the 1950's, Ray Charles struggled to make it in Florida. After three years of no progress he asked his guitar player to look at a map of the United States, "What's the furthest point from here?" he asked. It was Seattle. They went there. The rest is, as they say, history. In some circles they call this a geographic cure. If you have heard that phrase before, this may not be your solution.

You hate working alone? Get a partner. You hate your partner? Work alone. A small change might make a big difference and put the fun back in your act. Then you can keep at it. Here is Calvin Coolidge's famous quote on the subject.

Persistence

Nothing in the world can take the place of persistence.
Talent will not do it.
Nothing is more common
Than an unsuccessful man with talent.
Genius will not.
Unrewarded genius is almost a proverb.
Education will not.
The world is full of educated derelicts.
Persistence and determination alone are omnipotent.
The slogan—"Press On"—has solved, and always will solve,
The problems of the human race.

BUSINESS

15
How Do I Get The Big Break?

Big breaks are rare. A hundred little breaks are easier to get. The best way to get them is to be where breaks of all sizes are likely to occur. This means you are out often doing your act wherever they will have you. Go to seminars where people who have already succeeded will accept your money to tell you how they did it. At industry gatherings there are gatekeepers, agents, artists and promoters who will tell you everything for free if you ask.

Here is a self-test for your break potential. If you are alone most of the time, breaks are rare. If you can name the principal characters and plots of the latest TV shows, breaks are rare. If the last time you wrote a thank-you letter was on your birthday breaks are rare. If, in any conversation, you talk more than fifty percent of the time, breaks are rare. If you have not met somebody new today, breaks are rare. If you think that success is all in who you know, you might have a chance.

16
How Much Should I Charge?

"What is your fee?" A client asked.
"I would like to get about $200," I said.
"How about $300," he replied.
"I'm sorry, I thought you said $300," I said.
"I did," he said.
I accepted the gig, and thanked him for his generosity.
"Always glad to help," he said.
I remembered him in my prayers that night. The usual scenario is more like this:
"How much will this cost?"
"I charge $200 for two sets."
"OK. That's fine." Whereupon you think something like: *'Darn! There was more on the table, I wonder what I could have gotten?'* Here is the best way to do this.
"How much do you charge?"

"My fee varies according to how many sets, travel costs, and the night of the week. What is your budget?" They will either tell you a number, or be coy and say that it has not been worked out yet. If they give you a number, double it. "My normal fee is *(their doubled number)*."

"Oh! We can't afford that much!" Now you are negotiating. You can ask for reduced playing time in exchange for a lower fee, or expense re-imbursement, a nice dressing room, food, or whatever they can provide to make up for you charging less. You still might get something more than their original number. If they are coy, the dance has begun.

"I understand. Well, for four sets on a Saturday night, in... *(A city center far away)* my fee is... *(A big number you are comfortable with)*.

I have a consultant friend. His number is $10,000 for a day of fieldwork, a one-hour speech, and a written report a month later. He sometimes gets it. More often they blanche and say, "Our budget is only $3,500," which is what he wants anyway, and graciously agrees to if they can supply things like: First class air? Hotel suite? Signing privileges? My wife, too?

Back to the coy client. "Are you, nuts? That's way too much."

"Maybe we can work something out. What do you usually pay?"

You have put your cards on the table; now, usually, they will, too. Start high and settle reluctantly, but graciously, for less. Never give a range: "I get between $150 and $450, depending..." They will never hear anything but the low number. Do not be insulted by a low offer. If you cannot take the gig, refer them to someone you know who might, and will do an OK job. You have made a friend who has gigs. Get their telephone number and address. Send a follow-up letter saying how nice it was for them to call and maybe you will work together on another occasion.

17
What Goes Into A Press Kit?

Your picture: An 8 x 10 professional headshot. You may include a couple of poses on one 8 x 10 B&W glossy so that the editor can pick one, or both, to run.

Your bio: One page, wide margins. You may include everything on one page. See my bio and picture at the end of the book, for example.

This saves you money if a complete press kit is not required but you still want to give the full picture of the wonder that is you. However, a high quality B&W photo is required if you want the press to print a picture.

Your demo: CDs are required for airplay but you can use tapes to solicit gigs. A great live tape is best.

Your press. Press/Radio/TV highlights: If famous people have said nice things about you, then lead off your bio with the best three. If you have pages of glowing local press, you could make a big fat book out of it all. I have seen this done, and the sheer volume is impressive. Conversely, the cover of *TIME* or *Rolling Stone* would be all you need if you have it.

Do not include lyric sheets, or long lists of places you have played. If you have played a prestigious venue, like Carnegie Hall, that juicy bit should be in your bio. Do not waste money on printed glossy folders. A plain white one will do.

18
How Do I Write My Bio?

Do not write it yourself. What *you* write is a detailed history of who you are, where you came from, and where you are now. Be specific. For example, *I love to cook* is boring. While, *I cook Middle Eastern food. Baklava—pour the honey on while it's hot—and rolled grape leaves— cooked in oil, not steamed—are my specialties,* is interesting. It might run several typed pages.

Give this to a writer, preferably someone who knows you and your act but is not a big pal. A little distance will make for a better bio. The writer will condense your epic into a one-page bio packed with interesting detail and things you might not write about yourself.

If you must write it yourself, wear two hats. First, you are the free-form expounder on all that was, is, and will be you, you in the flesh, as it were. Then you become the brutal editor/writer who wants only the bone and sinew.

19
How Do I Get Publicity?

Publicity is advertising you do not pay for. To illustrate, here is the parable of The Naked Folksinger.

Bill Jones, singer/songwriter, struggles to get gigs in Boston. He has a good voice, a professional demo, and audiences seem to like him well enough. He is finding it hard to get noticed, however, and is at the end of the line with bookers, agents, and managers. When he calls for gigs it is tough to get through. If he gets through, he has a hard time generating any interest, "Send me your stuff. I'll have a look," is the usual response. It is like mailing to a black hole.

One day, at ten in the morning he calls the Lifestyle Editor of every newspaper in Boston. He calls the Boston office of national publications. He calls all the radio and TV stations in Boston. He says, "Today in Harvard Square at 5:00 PM, The Naked Folksinger will perform songs of life and love in support of *"Be Natural, Be Naked Week."* Bill made up this event. He sends everybody a follow-up press release via fax.

At 5:00 PM, Bill appears in Harvard Square with a few homemade signs. He modestly disrobes, straps on his guitar, and begins his act. A crowd gathers. A few media people gather. The police gather. Bill is arrested. Bill gets on the news. The next day, Bill holds a press conference. He is amusing, prepared, and entertaining; and he is in the news again.

Now when Bill calls for gigs he says, "Hello, this is The Naked Folksinger calling." Not Bill the faceless singer with an act sort of like everybody else.

"Hey, it's The Naked Folksinger. I saw you on TV."

"You're that guy who sang naked in Harvard Square!"

Bill has a brand name. He will register that brand name, get a trademark, and an Internet domain name. He will put a press kit together that has news value. He will send it—after calling first—to radio stations, clubs, agents and managers. He will lead with his brand name. People have heard of that brand name by virtue of free publicity. Bill got that free publicity by working the system. Here endeth the parable.

John Lennon and Yoko Ono appeared naked on the album cover, *Two Virgins*, thirty years ago. They gave a naked press conference in their bedroom. Although they were already famous, they had a cause—world peace—they wished to bring attention to.

You do not have to be naked. You do have to be newsworthy. Is there something about you that the media can use as a *hook?* Tell them what it is. After you have hooked them, make sure you have a story that you can deliver when they arrive. This is your *schtick,* as it was called in the Catskills. After reading about you, seeing you, and hearing you, people should be able to complete the following sentence:

"Suzie Smith? She's the one who *(insert your pithy positive description here)."* People will do this to you whether you like it or not, presuming they say anything. You do it, too. Lead them in the direction you want. Give them something they will remember about you that is newsworthy and, well, memorable. If your hook is that you admired this singer growing up, and you went to that school, and you wrote your first song about such and such, and you always wanted to be in show biz, and you're just so pleased to be here... Well, it does not get any more boring than that. "Please, you are making my eyes water..." as Don Imus would say. It is amazing how many people put this kind of material out as publicity background.

Get a hook. Be original. Tell everyone about it. Keep telling them the same thing.

20
What Makes A Good Concert Poster?

An arresting graphic that commands attention from a distance is the first and most important element. Movie and concert posters do this. Unless you are well known or extremely good-looking, your picture may not be that arresting graphic. Once you have their attention then tell who, what, where, when, and how much.

Use color. If your budget will not permit color printing, consider some hand coloring in bold strokes. Color commands attention.

Rock concert promoter Bill Graham commissioned established graphic artists to produce posters for his concerts. Works of artists like Bob Masse, www.bmasse.com, are now collectible[6].

21
Why Is Networking Important?

Songwriter Stephony Smith accepted the 1998 Country Music Award for song of the year, *It's Your Love*. She thanked Tom, who had introduced her to Dick, who passed the demo on to Harry, who gave it to Bill, who thought it was so good he called a friend of the recording artist who knew her producer. The producer played it for the singer who eventually sang the song and had the hit. Ms. Smith said she had been writing songs for twenty years and it felt pretty darn good to "...finally be standing here." Without that crowd of people to help get her songs heard, it may have taken even longer.

You are unique. You are talented. There are a thousand people as unique and talented. People choose to do business with people they know. You must know someone. They have to like you and you them. Then you can do some business. Since you cannot know in advance who will be that final golden connection to success, you meet as many people as you can and treat them all the same: like guardian angels.

Networking has taken some abuse lately. Some think if you show up somewhere for no other reason than to make some contacts, then you are somehow abusing the system. This is not the case. When you arrive on

---

[6] Bob Masse is from Canada's West Coast and has been producing concert posters since the 1960s. While attending art school in Vancouver, British Columbia he created posters for the folk acts that came through town in exchange for free drinks, tickets, and the opportunity to meet the musicians. Folk evolved into folk-rock with the Grateful Dead, The Doors, Jefferson Airplane and Steve Miller. In the late 1960s he spent time in Los Angeles and San Francisco where the art and music scenes influenced his work and is now avidly sought by collectors. Today, Bob continues to produce pieces for performers such as Alanis Morissette, Jimmy Buffett, Tori Amos, and Smashing Pumpkins.

any scene, you have brought value to the party. You bring yourself, your knowledge, and your experience. Someone is going to meet and learn from you, and you from them. Life is a contact sport. Go make some.

22
Should I Have A Website?

A website is a low cost electronic brochure. The main ways people learn about you are still concerts, print, radio, and TV. A web site is like a magazine or TV show devoted to you. It will not be of much interest until you have a fan base that wants to know about you. Then they will seek you out via your domain name: YOU.COM. You can also think of it as an electronic business card that you point people to via your other means of connecting with them. Do not lose your perspective. How excited were you when your name appeared in the phone book for the first time? Right now, it is not much different.

23
How Do I Set-Up A Website?

Register your name as in *steverapson.com*. There are many sites on the Internet where you can do this. **www.internic.net** is where you search to see if the name you want is available. **www.glassdog.com** is a site that makes this easy and entertaining. Register your domain name with Internic, also called Network Solutions, Inc. They will send you a bill, or you can pay on-line with a credit card. It costs $35 per year. Other sites will do all this for you for a fee, in addition to the $35. A web site designer will put your pages together and help you open an Internet account. If you cannot afford to have someone do this for you, there are books on the subject at any bookstore or at Amazon.com. In addition, on-line services like AOL make it very easy to set up a personal home page as part of their membership service.

24
Should I Try To Get A Patron?

Elvis had The Colonel. Claude Debussy had a rich sponsor support him until he earned his own way, as did Tarrega, the founder of the modern classical guitar method. Somebody with resources might like you and want to support your efforts and/or you while you are getting your start. Most people expect something in return for their contribution. Be careful what you agree to if you accept money, or anything, in exchange for a leg up.

25
What Organizations May I Join?

If more than three people are doing something, there is an organization of them to further the doing. Look for their newsletter or magazine, workshops and seminars. Join them all. Stay with the ones that you like; drop the ones you do not.

ASCAP — American Society of Composers, Authors and Publishers. www.ascap.com (800) 952-7227
ASMAC — American Society of Music Composer and Arrangers (818) 994-4661
BMI — Broadcast Music, Inc, www.bmi.com (310) 659-9109, (212) 586-2000
SESAC — www.sesac.com (800) 826-9996
NAS — National Academy of Songwriters. (800) 826-7287
NSAI — Nashville Songwriters Association International www.songs.org (800) 321-6008
NARAS — National Academy of Recording Arts & Sciences www.grammy.com
Just Plain Folks — www.jpfolks.com — Songwriter group.

Jason Blume's book, *6 Steps to Songwriting Success,* has a complete list of organizations, publications, and competitions in the appendix.

26
How Do I Find A Good Manager?

In the beginning you mange it all. Among your family and friends there may be someone who is pre-sold on you and has the desire and skills to manage your budding career.

A good manager loves you, loves your act, and never gets tired of talking about you. He carries a picture of you in his wallet. Your demo tape is always on in the car. He will kill for you. Every waking moment is turned towards how to get you that next big deal. He has little experience or contacts, but nothing will stop him while breath is in his body.

Or… A good manager has ten acts in his stable. Five of them have a top ten hit right now. Two are nominated for Grammys. With one telephone call, his newest act—maybe you—could be opening on tour for (*name of huge act goes here*). However, his time is taken with a hundred items a day. He is spread thin. There is so much to do. He says, "…and you are?" when you call. You decide whom to woo.

27
What Will A Manager Do For Me?

A personal manager is your head cheerleader. You are the CEO (Chief Executive Officer) of You, Inc. Your manager is the COO (Chief Operating Officer). In the beginning you and your manager do it all. Later, he helps pick your team: a lawyer, an agent, and an accountant

A personal manger helps develop your career: where to work, who to work with, what to charge? He helps you in the creative process. Is your act the best it can be, with the right songs and the right band? He works with agents to get the best gigs and help put itineraries together.

He plays bad cop when necessary. As when your record company ignores you, if you are lucky enough to *have* a record company to ignore you, allowing you to be just so darn nice all the time. Go to www.janisian.com. Janis Ian's articles about the music business are excellent and entertaining. Her articles on managers and mistakes are worth the trip.

28
What Do I Pay A Manager?

The usual deal is 15% of everything you earn for three to five years. There are many variations (such as, is it 15% of the gross or net?) Get a few books on the subject, such as *All You Need To Know About The Music Business*, by Donald Passman and Ronald Zalkind's *Getting Ahead in the Music Business*.

29
Should I Sign A Management Contract?

The only performers without managers are those with no career to manage. The trick is to have an act of sufficient quality to interest somebody in managing you. Talent helps but it is not sufficient. You need an established record of accomplishment such as fans that come to see you and buy your tapes, or CDs, or books.

Most managers need to make money after signing you. If all you are doing is coffeehouses at $50 a gig, there is not much there for anyone else. Every act starts at that level. You hope to move on quickly so that you can hire a manager who will free you up to do what you do best.

Never sign anything without the help of an entertainment lawyer. It is a good idea to educate yourself first by reading books and talking to people who have done it already.

30
How Far Should I Travel For A Gig?

Half as far as you can afford to go. You have to get back. If it is a showcase for unsigned acts, with major record labels in the audience, you might want to borrow the money to fly across the country. If it is a standard bar gig, walking across the street and unpacking your guitar may seem like too much work.

When you begin, a good strategy is to get a map and draw a circle around your home base. It should have a one to two hundred mile radius. This is the limit of how far you can drive, do the gig, and drive home. Now draw smaller circles inside. Say at ten, twenty-five, fifty miles, and so on. Start with the inner circle. Identify all the places within that circle that may be a good place for you to work and concentrate on just those venues. Build your audience from the inside out.

When I started my band I used the Yellow Pages. I looked up Clubs, Associations, and Restaurants, identified locals by the exchanges and called the ones closest to me. I landed regular work with a nearby golf club and dance club. I also called prospects further out. When the far away ones turned into regulars, I appreciated how much better it was to work close to home.

31
Are Travel Expenses Reimbursed?

Everything is negotiable, and it does not hurt to ask. However, the lower you are on the entertainment food chain, the less there is to eat.

32
Should I Fire My Manager?

Yes, if you are not happy, unless you have signed a five-year deal with no performance or escape clauses. That is when you wish you had paid $300 to that lawyer before you signed.

33
Do I Need An Agent?

If you want good gigs you need an agent. Good agents, the ones with the good gigs, are not interested in you until you hit a certain income and recognition level. Club managers and local booking agents are where you have to start. After a buzz gets going, you get a manager. Then your manager finds an agent. Then your agent gets you a headliner spot at a national event. Then you become a star. Who said this was hard?

Pretty Polly Productions, a leading Boston agency, occasionally booked my band. For the first few years, however, I did all the booking myself. Until our name was known, we did not earn enough to make it worthwhile for the agent.

34
What Do I Pay An Agent?

Franchised music business agents get you gigs at concerts, club dates, festivals, commercials, and on TV. They get a 10% commission on the money you earn from this work. They are not paid from money you might earn selling records or books, unless, for some reason, you agree to this. Franchised agents are big players. They abide by union rules. Small, local agencies may charge up to 15% and are free to work with non-union acts.

© 2000 The New Yorker Collection from cartoonbank.com. All Rights Reserved.

"No, Thursday's out. How about never—is never good for you?"

35
Does Cold Calling Work To Get Gigs?

Yes. In addition to cold calling, show up where you want to work. Observe who is who and what the scene is. Talk to everybody, especially those who have gigs there. Compliment them, and ask about their act. Beware of telling too much about yourself. People with social skills will ask about you. Keep your answer short, and then ask more about them. Make a connection with people by showing genuine interest in them and what they do. If they have something for sale, buy it: a CD, book, or T-shirt.

After you make a personal connection it is easier to ask, How did you get this gig? Who do I talk to? What are their requirements? Anything I should know, do's and don'ts? Show up. There is no other way. Ben Franklin said, "If you want a thing to be done, go. If not, send."

In Boston's suburbs, a local Air Force Officer's Club threw great New Year's Eve parties. One year, I abandoned Rosemary to schmooze with the band on their break. The guitarist told me they drove from South

Carolina for this gig, with their travel expenses picked up by the Club. They were a competent band, but I knew we could do as well. I got the manager's name by chatting with a bartender. He said, "Harold is here now. Did you want to see him about something?" Sure, I said. He escorted me to the manager's office, "What can I do for you?" Harold said. I complimented him on the great party and the great band. He jumped right in and said, "That band is costing me a fortune. The one I hired cancelled at the last minute and this was the only one the agent could get on short notice." I handed him my card, and said I would be in touch and thanked him again for the party. I followed up with a letter. That meeting turned into dozens of gigs over several years.

The most productive cold call I ever made was to the manager of a golf club. He hired us immediately, and we eventually became the club's house band. It made the hundreds of rejections worthwhile.

36
What Is The Music Business Jungle?

It is where most acts live their musical lives. Music business author, Ronald Zalkind, says the jungle is everything outside of the legitimate music business. In the jungle there are no record deals, managers, agents, or contracts. It is a world of bad gigs, low money, and sub-par musicians. Your mission is to exit the jungle and return only on brief safaris. Zalkind's book, *Getting Ahead in the Music Business,* is less technical than Passman's, *All You Need To Know About The Music Business,* but no less accurate.

37
How Do I Find Promoters?

Usually you do not want to deal with promoters yourself. This is the agent's job. If you are just getting started, and no agent will talk to you, there are small promoters in every city. They run ads for acts they are promoting in the entertainment listings of major and minor papers.

They put out flyers. Collect these ads and flyers; note the concerts and venues that have acts similar to yours. The promoter is usually listed in the ad. Call those promoters to see if you can submit a press kit and be an opening act, or be part of a review. It takes at least six calls to get a callback or to get through. Be nice, be patient. When you get semi-famous, promoters will start calling you.

38
How Do I Choose The Best Venue?

I was hired for a Friday/Saturday gig at a local bar. My act was for listening. The audience wanted line dancing to the Bee Gees. I did not go over. Before the night was finished, the bartender called me over and said, "Here's your money for the night, you can go now, and we won't need you tomorrow." It felt bad at the time, but he did me a favor.

Ideally, when you perform, you have the opportunity to show your strengths, sign up new people, and sell CDs. An acoustic act that needs a quiet room and full attention may not work in all venues. If you play a corner bar with fifty people more interested in drinking than in listening, you do not go over. Fifty people see you not going over. In a different environment, many of these people might have become your fans. Instead you have created a first impression in their minds of an act that is not cutting it. If you do one of these gigs a week, in a year you create thousands of negative first impressions within your market. A basic marketing principle is to know your customer and know your product. Identify who your audience is, where they are, and how your product must be presented.

My friend and producer, Steven Friedman, says you start out at open mikes where there are ten people in the room, nine of whom hate your act. Eventually, you open for an act with a small following. There are a hundred people in the room and ninety of them hate you. You persist and land an afternoon spot at a big festival. There are a thousand people on the grass, and nine hundred of them do not like you one tiny bit, but a hundred do. A hundred people in a dozen cities is the beginning of a bona fide career as a performer. Mr Friedman concludes that the key to success is to get a lot of people to hate your act.

39
The Ten Commandments of Recording
by Steven Friedman[7]

I. **Knowest Thy Purpose**—Be clear on why you are making the recording and on what you intend to do with it. Artists often waste a lot of time and money because they do not know what they want, and therefore do not know what to do or when to stop.

II. **Thou Shalt Not Expect Too Much From Thy Recordings**—Your career depends on your song writing, playing & singing skills, gigging, stage presentation, booking, promotion, publicity, distribution, and contacts. An album is only part of the picture.

III. **Thou Shalt Not Overspend**—Promotion, distribution, gigging, and travel cost money. Spending it all on recording is like buying a Ferrari and not having anything for gas.

IV. **Thou Shalt Not Interrupt Thy Career Whilst Recording**—Disappear into the studio for six months and nobody will remember you when you emerge. Do not stop writing and gigging.

V. **Thou Shalt Not Rehearse In The Studio**—If you cannot play it in your bedroom, you will not be able to play it in the studio.

---

[7] Steve Friedman holds a Ph.D. in Physics. He worked at MIT before starting his own recording studio.

VI. **Thou Shalt Not Confuse Thy Friends With Studio Musicians**—You think your pals sound great jammin' in your kitchen. Put them under the microscope of a studio mixdown session and you may be in for a shock.

VII. **Thou Shalt Not Try To Be Thine Own Engineer**—Self-recording is a good way to prepare for a project, but a bad way to do one. I have seen artists spend a year making an album at home that could have been made better in one day at my studio.

VIII. **Thou Shalt Not Expect More Than Thou Payest For**—Cheap recordings sound cheap.

IX. **Lay Thy Tribute At The Altar of Time, And Not At The Altar of Fancy Gear**—If your budget is limited, it's better to pay for a lot of time at a modest studio with rates you can comfortably afford, than to rush and cut corners at a state-of-the-art studio with a high hourly rate.

X. **Thou Shalt Remember To Enjoy Thyself**—Success in the music business is so rare it is foolish to even try if you are not having fun.

40
How Do I Make A Video?

Video demos are much like audio demos except they are about ten times harder to do, and cost about that much more, too. You need a funded budget, an experienced producer, and a specific objective for

Jeo. Otherwise you are just playing around. Consider Access TV as a resource for an entry-level video project. cable company can help with equipment and crew.

41
How Do I Interest A Record Company?

Red Motley, legendary salesman and former Chairman of Parade Magazine, said:
"Know your product, know your customer, see a lot of people, and ask all to buy."
When you are writing and performing, you are doing what you want to do. Everything else is sales, marketing, distribution, and promotion, none of which you may want to do. Performers need agents and managers, record companies and distribution companies. What record companies want is originality, according to Karin Berg talent scout for Warner Brothers Records. Major labels might spend a million dollars to break a new artist nationally. Smaller labels may spend proportionally less, but it is still serious commitment. It is a bet they may win or lose. Sony Music President Thomas Mottola signed Mariah Carey a few days after he was handed her unlabelled tape. Later he married her. This is the exception. Ten thousand albums are released each year. Sixteen percent sell more than ten thousand units the first year. Eighty percent of all CDs released in a year sell less than ten thousand copies. Not all of them represent a one million-dollar investment. However, they all cost something and most do not make their costs back.
Even if you are a star, if your records stop selling, you will not have a record company. 1980's pop star Chris Cross started in Texas playing college frat houses. In addition to cover songs, his band did Chris' originals. He sent demos to agents, record companies and radio stations. He made thousands of telephone calls, he wrote hundreds of letters. He saw everybody. He knew the movers and shakers in Texas, and they knew of him. He got signed. He won song of the year (1980—*Sailing*). Later, he wrote and recorded the title song to the movie *Arthur*. Then his popularity waned. His record company dropped him. He is not poor, and if he tours, he has a solid base of fans who will fill a small venue. That is a typical path through the music business. At the beginning and at the end you do many things for yourself.

I am my own record company. I have five CDs in release, global distribution at Amazon.com and MusicDude.com, and monthly advertising in *Acoustic Guitar Magazine*. Most of my sales are at performances with mail order and Internet orders small but steady.

I had researched other guitarists' work and felt there was room for me in the world of acoustic solo guitarists. In addition, those sales statistics convinced me that I could sell enough to be profitable. Even if I sold only a thousand CDs, I would still be in the same order of magnitude as 84% of all CDs released in the US. I also produce transcription books of my original songs and those in the public domain. It is satisfying to be in charge of the business side, as well as the creative.

Until you have a team to do the things you do not want to do, follow Red's advice.

42
What Good Are Testimonials?

They are the best form of advertising. It is the way you get known, especially in the beginning. Don White says, "I want to write and perform in such a way that the next day people who were at my show will grab their co-workers by the shoulders and say, *'You have got to hear this guy.'* "

Ask for them. When I sell or give away a CD, I say, "If you like it, please drop me a note and tell me what you liked about it." I also say, "If it is not your cup of tea, you don't have to tell me that." You will get three or four testimonials for every hundred you ask for. So ask for many. The best ones become part of your press kit, your advertising, and the buzz about you.

Testimonials are the best form of advertising because they are impossible to fake. You can always tell a shill from a real person. It is that innate sense of the truth we all have. We sense we are hearing the real deal with a testimonial.

43
Can I Make A Living Entertaining?
By Don White

Let us begin with the premise that the music industry is a big, hairy, evil monster that eats its young and that the odds against anyone surviving, let alone making a living from, their relationship with it are substantial. Now that we have established a portrait of the industry, let us talk numbers.

I have been in the Boston singer-songwriter scene for ten years. In that time I have known three or four hundred people who have tried, or are still trying, to make a living performing. Sixty percent of these people are gone. The industry devoured them quickly and with surprisingly little effort.

Half of the remaining forty percent are still playing open mikes. They are not building any audience or making any real money. Many of the people in this group are not trying to make a living at music. They continue to do it because they love it. Their performances are always fun and fulfilling for them and the pressure of the biz never weighs them down. These people are smarter than the rest of us.

Of the remaining twenty percent roughly half are musicians who diversified to stay in the business. They may run a recording studio, work in radio, do live sound engineering, be newspaper critics, or freelance writers. They may run a club or coffeehouse, do CD or cassette duplication, or any combination of these in addition to live performing. This pragmatic group has made decisions that enable them to stay in and around the business and perform at least some of the time.

The final ten-percent can be broken into two groups. Eight percent are the people with a small record deal, some radio airplay, a growing audience, and reasonable prospects for success. These are the road warriors. They live in their automobiles. When you talk to them, they are spacy and distant. They try to focus on your face but all they can see are white lines from the highway. They try to listen to you, but your words are muffled by the permanent hum of tires on asphalt burned into their minds. These people play a lot of gigs for amounts of money that cannot cover the cost of getting there, with the assumption that eventually it will pay off. For some of them it will.

The remaining two percent are the ones who are generating enough income to perhaps pay a mortgage on a small house and have a new or at least a decent car. Being able to afford a house and a car is not an outrageous expectation for most working Americans, but in the singer/songwriter world this represents a rare and inspirational accomplishment.

I am not trying to discourage you. However, it is important to have a realistic view of what you are up against so you can prioritize, consolidate your resources, and apply the appropriate energy.

44
Should I Do Cable Access TV Shows?

Yes. It is easy and it is free. Call your cable company. Ask who is in charge of community television. They will tell you how to get on TV. They exist for the sole purpose of helping you be on TV.

Do not let your expectations get out of hand, however. I have done dozens of local cable TV shows. One night at Java Jo's Coffeehouse, a teenager said to me, "Didn't I see you on TV at 3:00AM on a cable channel that nobody watches?" Yes! That was me. Want my autograph?

It may seem insignificant, but Barry Nolan (ex-*Hard Copy*) said, "Either you are on the bus or you are not on the bus." The bus is Barry's metaphor for the camera pointing in your direction. Which is why you will see stars like Whoopie Goldberg and Luther Vandross on Hollywood Squares. Get on the bus. Get on TV

45
Should I Start A Mailing List?

Your mailing list is the engine that propels your career. Get everyone you meet to sign up. Robert Allen, author of *Nothing Down*, says each name on your mailing list is worth an average of one dollar per year in income to you.

Enlist the help of fans in selling your tapes, CDs, posters, T-shirts. Anyone who shows interest in you gets on your mailing list. For the first five hundred names you will do all the stuffing and licking yourself. After that, you will need a mailing service company to handle it for you.

Your mailing list needs attention. A clean list has no dead addresses. It is not littered with people who have not bought a single thing from you. If you send a 500-postcard mailer announcing your big concert and the only people who show up are your mother and your significant other, then that list is not working for you.

46
Should I Have A Newsletter?

When you have news, and a list of people who care, do a newsletter. You can use it to sell your products, announce your concerts, and tell interesting stories of your successes so far.

Include a profile of one or two of your fans. Have a fan write about how he or she promotes you. Eventually your fans will do the newsletter. Include them in the news about you.

47
How Do I Get My Next Gig?

Ask for another gig where you had your last gig. It is much easier to sell an existing customer than to find a new customer. The single most important thing you can do to sell more to your existing customer is to say, "Thank you." Say it in writing every time you have any dealings with that customer. Even if they say, "No, go away." No means *no for now*, not *no forever*. Be specific in your thanks. Tell your customer exactly what their business means to you.

This is obvious you say? Perhaps it is. But so few people do it that when you do it, you will rise out of the sea of fellow performers like a shining beacon on the rocks of unexpressed gratitude. Let me give you some numbers.

From May 1994 to December 1997 I booked acoustic entertainment for a small coffeehouse south of Boston. During that time I booked an average of one hundred and fifty acts each year. In three and half years I hired nearly five hundred performers. What percentage of these acts do you think sent a thank-you note? Ten percent? That would be fifty notes of thanks. Not that many. In fact, I received less than ten. It was so few that I can still remember the first and last name of each person who sent a note, no reference material required. Less than two percent. Be remembered. Be a pro. Say thanks.

48
What Products Can I Sell At Gigs?

CDs, Tapes, T-shirts, hats, autographed photos, dolls that look like you, coloring books of you saving the rain forest. Give away free pens, pencils, stickers, and refrigerator magnets. If it is cheap and you can print your name on it, do it and give it away. Singer/songwriter Ratsy is famous for her ubiquitous stickers. She will send you some free if you send her a SASE. Go to www.ratsy.com

49
Who Should Sell For Me?

You are the best sales person. After the show, help sell your stuff. During your show, ask a trusted person from the club, or a member of your crew.

Your fans want to meet you. This is a good way to do it. Have a Sharpie pen and autograph your tapes and CDs books, whatever you are selling.

I attended a Penn & Teller magic show. After the finale Messrs. P & T ran down the aisle. As we filed out, there they were in the lobby behind a big table selling their stuff. They talked, signed and sold for over an hour. Be like them.

50
How Do I Sell From The Stage?

If you are funny you can make your pitch part of the act. Don White does a funny bit linking CD sales to spousal rewards when he gets home. In general, I would be careful about selling too much from the stage. You are there to entertain. It is appropriate to hold up your latest CD or book and say it is available, and that you would be happy to sign it for anyone who wishes, and thank-you for your support. Beyond that let the host or MC pitch for you.

51
What Is A Song Plugger?

Someone who pitches your songs for a fee. That fee may be a monthly retainer, a percentage if they succeed, or a combination. The best song pluggers are difficult to hire, just like the best managers, lawyers, and agents. You must go looking for them and sell them on your songs.

52
What Is A Song Shark?

A phony song plugger who earns money by extracting up-front fees from you, rather than succeeding in selling your songs. There are many more sharks than pluggers out there. They come looking for you.

MATERIAL

© 2000 The New Yorker Collection from cartoonbank.com. All Rights Reserved

*"And that was my day at the office. Thanks, Alice,
you've been a great audience!"*

53
Where Do I Get Appropriate Material?

Reveal yourself. Your shortcomings are most interesting. We try to hide our faults from others and may not be fully aware of them ourselves. Clear-eyed self-appraisal is required. Little tragedies in our lives are a source, if not of humor, then an interesting anecdote. It is easier to talk about bad things that have happened to you after time has passed. You will see the humor or a moral. Write them out as a brief *by the way* anecdote. I recommend Judy Carter's, *Stand-Up Comedy: The Book* to see how this is done. Here is one of mine:

Introduce it: *"Thought I got a ticket in a parking lot... It was just one of those flyers they put on all the cars."*

Set it up: *"It said, 'We are looking for 15 overweight men'."* (wait...)

Pay it off: (pantomime looking around...) *"I was the only one with a flyer."*

I was not amused when this happened. I have since pared it down, practiced my timing, and now it is funny. Self-deprecating humor is easy and people love you for it. In addition to prepared material, leave room in your act for spontaneous risk-taking. This *overweight men* bit was first a spontaneous aside. You will develop a keen sense for this sort of thing. When something bad happens to you, your next thought, after "Ouch!" could be, "Oh, boy! A new bit!"

Folk singer Tom Rush tells of the time he saw Josh White break a guitar string. Josh kept playing and singing while he changed the string. A virtuoso performance, said Tom. The audience shouted and clapped their approval. The next night, Tom happened to be in the audience again. Josh broke the same string during the same song. He did the string change with the same result. A little suspicious, Tom stopped in a third night and you know what happened. At some past gig Josh White accidentally broke a string and did his best to keep the show going. He got a great, unexpected reaction. Josh made sure he broke a string at every show after that.

As a performance coach I have heard the following many times:

"It's not me to do an 'act'. It seems so phony. I want to be real with the audience. I just say whatever I feel at the time. It's no fun for me, and I think the people don't like it, either, if I say the same thing I said the night before. I mean, what if they were in the audience then, too?"

There is nothing wrong if you just walk out, say 'Hello', sing your songs, end with 'Thank you very much' and exit." Martin Sexton does this. He told me once that he can't do the stage banter thing, wishes he could, and is totally envious of those who have an act apart from their singing and song writing. If you are blessed with a three-octave set of pipes like Mr. Sexton, little else is required to succeed in this business. Most of us need an act.

54
Is It Ethical To Use Another Performer's Material?

No. This is not to say that performers do not borrow liberally from each other. If you lift directly from someone else, then give attribution. If you adopt something that you revise to fit you and your persona, that is a gray area. Let your conscience be your guide.

Your act will start out with much inadvertent or ill-advised borrowing. As you progress, you will displace the borrowed material with your own.

55
Should I Use Only My Own Material?

If you are a singer, or storyteller, or give speeches that others have written, then your job is to pick material that resonates with you, fits your persona, and is entertaining. Frank Sinatra was the greatest pop singer of our century. He did not write a thing, yet he sang every song as if he had written it.

Comedian Lenny Bruce's first big break was in October, 1948 on the Arthur Godfrey Talent Scouts show. He performed a variation of a Red Buttons' bit called *The Bavarian Mimic*. Early Bruce shows also included his mother's routines. His mother Sadie Kitchenberg, was a small-time comedy figure who went by the stage names Sally Marr and Boots Malloy. A club owner told Sadie, "Do you know Lenny is going around doing your act?" She was flattered, but told Lenny he had to write his own material if he wanted to get anywhere.

56
Should I Pay For Material?

If you are speaking, give attribution to those you quote. If you are singing, ASCAP or BMI have systems to collect and distribute the money for use of other people's songs at a club or concert.

If you are recording, then you or your record company must pay the Harry Fox Agency (212-834-0100 or www.harryfox.com) for the right to use someone else's song. This is called a compulsory mechanical license. It is compulsory because the copyright holder cannot refuse you a license to record a previously released song.

57
Where Can I Find Good Jokes?

The best material arrives by surprise. Earl Nightingale said, "Ideas are like slippery fish, you must gaff them with the point of a pencil before they slip away."

Avoid shaggy dog stories: those long set-ups with poor, or corny, punch lines. Nobody likes them. Similarly, lawyer jokes, ethnic jokes, or off-color jokes rarely work unless you are an experienced comedian and your audience has some expectation about your material. Find humor from your own life; write down potential bits as they happen to you and use them in your act.

I was the victim of an ironic surprise when one of my clients turned my advice around on me.

I coach Meghan, a woman who has a lovely way with a torch ballad, and occasionally accompany her on guitar. One night, we were sitting cheek by jowl, packed into Club Passim's Tuesday Open Mike. On stage, a pony-tailed, gray-haired bohemian man was buried in a Bob Dylan songbook, reading us the lyrics as if they were last week's meeting minutes.

I thought, *Could this be any lamer?*

Meghan tapped me on the shoulder and held up a note. It said, *"Crazy?"* I looked at the guy reading, leaned over and whispered, "That could explain it."

She looked puzzled, did a silent *ohhh,* and whispered, "I mean the song. Do you want to do *Crazy* with me?"

I nodded, blushing at my lack of charity exposed. As penance, I resolved to pay attention to the epic still unfolding. Now that I was listening, Dylan's brilliant writing drew me in. Mr. Crazy was hardly that. He was serious, committed, and had great material. In fact, were I to coach him, my only suggestion would be to get an opening that made know-it-all snobs like me pay attention sooner.

Later, it was our turn.

Meghan was the star. I was the sideman. She was a natural and took control of the stage with ease and grace. She began with a personal anecdote:

"Hi, everybody! Just before we came up I asked Steve, my guitarist, what we should play…" Meghan told the *Crazy* story. I hid behind her because Mr. Crazy was sitting in the front row, close enough to bite my toe if he had the inclination. No one would have blamed him.

I later explained to Meghan that stories of personal foibles have to be about how *you* looked silly, not me.

58
What Subjects Are Taboo On Stage?

During the open mike at Club Passim, a man sang about his backseat encounter with a woman. It was graphic and artless. The audience booed him soundly. Conversely, in the 1930's, Billie Holiday sang *Strange Fruit.* It is about lynching black people in the South. A

© 2000 The New Yorker Collection from cartoonbank.com. All Rights Reserved

*"The love ballad I'm about to sing will pose
a lot of uncomfortable questions about gender identity and
class-based issues. I hope you can handle it."*

haunting, beautiful song that is also tragic. Some subject might be off-limits, but if handled properly I believe anything can work.

Goddamn HIV was written by singer/songwriter Mary Gauthier. She sings it in the voice of a young man with AIDS, and never fails to grab the audience with her stark lyrics and bittersweet performance. Even the darkest of subjects lend themselves to skillful writing: violence against women, the sad memories of an adult sexually abused as a child, the death penalty; these are topics I have seen work in a song. Seattle singer/songwriter David Roth sings a breathtakingly funny song about *Special K* cereal. It was invented, he says, to control self-abuse in young men. He never used the word that rhymes with *infatuation.*

The difference between material that offends, and that which moves and connects, is where it eventually takes us. An audience will let you drag them through the muck and mire, but they will not be happy if you leave them there. They need a resolution, something that uplifts and informs about the human spirit. For example, this song:

Heartbeat of Heaven[8]
By Don White

Hello my friend it's me again.
I know I only show up when I'm all tore to shreds.
And so here I am. I'm a mess again
Standing in the doorway of my oldest friend.

You see my son got mugged down on Boston Street
They put a pistol to his temple and took his money
No, no he's OK. Tonight he's home and he's safe
But look at me I'm all in pieces again.

(chorus)
Jesus, please just hold me and cradle me near to your breast
With my head against the heartbeat of heaven
I know my poor heart can heal and rest.

The way I feel today I am so full of rage
If I could get near that mugger I could blow him away.
But when you cradle me my heart can always see
That hatred is the real mugger strangling me.
And my soul can't breathe with this weight on me.
Until I let it go, my soul won't know no peace

(chorus)

If this man I hate came to you today
The love you'd wrap around each of us would be the same.
That amazes me to see that love can be
Perfect, without judgment, constant and free.
As I live and breathe I truly do believe that no words can describe
What this love does for me.

Jesus please just hold me and cradle me near to your breast
With my head against the heartbeat of heaven
I know my poor heart can heal and rest.
I am going home now to heal and rest.

After Don sings this moving song he reads the following spoken piece. He tells about how his song connected with a woman in the

---

[8] From *Rascal* © Lyric Moon Records. Lyrics and Spoken Piece used by permission.

audience at one of his shows. Don does this because he knows that connecting with his audience is the reason he performs. He has the instinct and the ability to risk revealing himself, in humor or pathos, to connect with them. This is performance art of the highest level.

Spoken Piece

After the concert a woman stood in the theater until everyone was gone. When we were alone she asked about that song, "you know the one about your son getting mugged at gunpoint," was it true? There was a long pause and then she said, "My sixteen year old niece was just beaten to death by her girlfriend's ex-husband." The words came out of her as if they had made the decision to be spoken on their own and she seemed to me like an unwilling but helpless vehicle for their desire. They hung in the air between us for what seemed like a very long time and then moved slowly toward me and landed upon my back. This was among the heaviest of sentences I have ever shouldered and my knees immediately buckled beneath the weight of it. I had no words for this woman. This was one of those moments that shed light on the inherent inability of language to communicate adequately in matters of the heart.

She wound up in my arms. Holding her being an infinitely more eloquent expression of my complex emotions than any words I might have struggled to assemble. I was hoping that she would not address the obvious contrast in our experiences—namely, how much easier it was for me to sing about healing in regard to a situation that did not take the life of my loved one. When she eventually spoke she said that the event was recent and that she had been refusing to deal with it because it was so new and so horrible; but hearing my song made it impossible for her to keep the door closed to the wound in her heart and that she was actually coming to grips with the tragic magnitude of it for the first time. Holding this sad and beautiful woman during this moment in her life was overwhelming. I felt her heart crack and then shatter into pieces. I felt a cold wind blow through the hole in her chest which until that moment had been occupied by her warm and vital heart. Every three of four seconds her entire body shook uncontrollably as if someone were applying voltage to it. Inside my own emotional frame I was experiencing one of those outrageous moments where I find myself besieged by very powerful contradictory feelings occurring simultaneously. I felt awkward and inadequate. What could I possibly do for this woman? But I also felt extremely privileged to be involved in such a profound human interaction. My heart was heavy with sadness for the depth of her suffering—but I also felt that there was an undeniable solemn beauty to the moment. It was exhilarating. It was exhausting.

When she was gone, and I was left alone to ponder what had just transpired, I was immediately struck by how lucky I felt that I chose to write the song from a perspective of healing rather than any of the other points of view that an event like that imposes upon its victims. Anger, resentment, bitterness, revenge, helplessness and fear were all viable candidates for the theme of the song but I chose to write from my prayer place, which is where I go at the times in my life when I am in an emotional freefall. Where God's unconditional love can wrap its wings around me and breathe its eternal wisdom back into my scattered pieces. I knew that this was a place to write from that would enable me to give something positive to the listener as opposed to just emphasizing the obvious negative aspects of the incident.

What I learned from my short time with this woman is that in some instances language can be an entirely ineffective means of communication between human beings. In other instances it is capable of piercing the most heavily fortified armor that a person might assemble to protect their secrets, their vulnerabilities, or their pain. The close proximity of the subject matter of the song to this woman's recent tragedy was such that she could not defend herself against it. The song penetrated her defenses and laid bare the wound. Had it been full of the bitterness and anger that I felt at the time of the mugging, I would have been guilty of the very serious crime of laying my knife to the open wound of a stranger. And my expertise in this art of expression would have been the weapon with which I rendered this person helpless against this felony.

If we as writers are going to hone the blades of our craft so that they cut swiftly and indefensibly to the core of a given subject, we should not underestimate the immense responsibility that comes with this calling. If we are blessed with the rare and privileged ability to put our hands on the pain of strangers, we should live each moment with the knowledge that heaven will not shine gently upon the hand of any artist that touches the pain of her children with anything less than compassion and love.

59
Should My Act Be Scripted?

"**E**very word, every blink, every breath, every twitch." This according to David Letterman who told Charlie Rose the story of his big break. He was called to appear on the Tonight Show. He had several months to prepare six minutes of stand-up. He polished and tightened and practiced till he was a well-oiled machine. When Letterman's national debut arrived, it appeared as if he was speaking off the cuff, that one great line after another was just popping into his head.

When Robin Williams hosted a TV benefit for Christopher Reeve, he opened with his patented brand of spontaneous humor, running up and down the aisles and working the crowd. I forecasted punch lines to his spontaneous ad-libs, thoroughly annoying my family. Williams has been doing these same gags on national television since 1980. He still gets big laughs with well-written, well-rehearsed, old material.

Writing good new material is hard. Once you have it, then you work on timing and delivery. When you have something that works, you use it; and you do not change it… ever!

David and Robin are pros. Be like them.

60
How Topical Should I Be?

Life, Love, Death, Taxes. These are timeless topics. Great writing on these subjects will last your entire career. If you want to be topical in your songs and speaking, be prepared for extra writing. Material on the personalities and events of the day will be old almost by the time you are ready to perform it.

61
How Important Is Humor
To My Performance?

Humans are the only creatures who laugh. We can laugh at anything when presented appropriately. Singer/songwriter Mary Gauthier uses humor to lighten up the room after she sings three songs in a row about, respectively, alcoholism, family estrangement, and capital punishment. She says, "I guess this would be a good time for one of my happy songs, but I just played them all." It always works.

Christine Lavin is known for her humorous songs and sell-out performances. Her web site, www.christinelavin.com, has a collection of tips for beginning performers. They are an advanced course in successful stage work. I recommend it highly.

Self-deprecating humor is the easiest to do. Poke fun at yourself with a grin and everybody will smile and warm to you immediately. *"Leave them laughing when you go"* is an age-old commandment of the stage because people remember most what you did last. Even if you died a thousand deaths during your show, save a guaranteed funny bit to close. It saves the show, the day, and your career.

PERFORMANCE

62
What Are Open Mike Nights?

An open mike night is where you start. No matter what you do, in the beginning, you do it free anywhere you can. If you are a budding speaker, Toastmasters is the open mike night for you. You get a stage, a supportive audience, and five minutes.

Singer/songwriters, poets, and comics often share a stage, but usually they hang out at their own open mikes. Ann Eder-Mulhane tells how it was for her.

First Open Mike Feature
By Ann Eder-Mulhane[9]

"How would you like to feature?" asked host Steve Rapson as he sat down beside me at the metal topped table facing the stage at Java Jo's Coffeehouse. It was Wednesday night—Open Mike Night—and the air was steamy with coffee and music. I had just finished singing, eleventh out of twelve performers who had played. I almost spilled my coffee.

"Very much," was all I could manage, my insides flipping.

It was a long awaited moment. I had been at the very first Open Mike almost two years ago. I showed up each week from then on, beginning with a squeaking voice and strumming my guitar softly enough to hide my bad playing. I continued to come because I was fighting two strong convictions. One saying, 'You aren't nearly good enough', the other saying, 'You have something here, you have a strong rich offering'. One conviction makes me sweat, work, reach and practice; the other keeps me standing upright on the stage.

Two years later, I was still upright on stage. I had met some working musicians, some courageous blunderers, some players gifted with magic. I had grown to admire our loyal audience. I'd sung, messed up, strengthened, and watched with jealousy and resignation as some performers were featured after only a few months, others after their very first visit to Java Jo's. If I had not stayed, joining and supporting this varied and vibrant musical

---

[9] Ann is now the host of Java Jo's Open Mike in Milton, Massachusetts..

community, I would never have been offered a feature on a night in October.

At first, I thought all I had to do was show up and sing my heart out for half an hour. Luckily for me, though, I met with Steve for some coaching. Yes, I had to sing strongly, but I also learned I had to prepare a balanced program of six songs: one to catch fire with, some to show your strength and conviction as a songster, others to ease down and join with the audience. Steve taught me to practice everything I did on stage in front of the mirror: beginnings and endings, stage movements, bows, the position of the microphone, song introductions. I even had to learn not to fret about my weakness: guitar playing.

Then came the most important—and hardest—lesson of all: I had to learn to include the audience at all times. Think that sounds easy? Looking at them, noticing them, joining and thanking them with words and movements, body and eyes involves at lot of looking outward. For me, this meant translating the Spanish songs I sing and giving up that God-like stance that I thought kept me so cool on stage: singing to myself and to the skies while the audience sat raptly watching (I wished!).

I practiced for weeks, OK, for months. Then the night arrived. My huge family was there, my husband and son, many fellow musicians and some regular audience members. As Steve adjusted the mike I remembered to smile and keep my eyes on the audience. That was the last focused thought I had for the next half-hour. Which seems pitiful. The only part of me that felt strong was my voice. I admit I used that to cover the awkward jelly-like feeling in every part of me. I sang more and more. I noticed the audience less and less. Afterward a trusted friend said to me,

"What's the point of eating a gourmet meal if you don't have room to savor the taste and digest it all properly? Accept their applause, Dodo!"

A true friend!

My first feature was a powerful night for me. It showed me that my strengths still co-exist with my weaknesses: Although I can perform for a solid half-hour, I still have plenty to work on. I have not joined the ranks of Clapton or Segovia on guitar. However, my voice is stronger, my poise less meek. I have joined a remarkable community that is supportive and ever growing. In a pinch, I can always ask my friend Steve to tune my guitar.

I identify with Ann's story. After twenty years as a rock and roll bandleader, I quit music. Five years later, I returned as an acoustic player and budding singer songwriter. My debut was at the Olde Vienna

Kaffehaus. My friend Bob said, "Let's go to the Olde Vienna. It's a famous place and they have an open mike on Tuesday. You can sing your new songs."

God! I have not been to an open mike since I was a teenager. Open mikes are for beginners and the musically inept. This is not the case, but I was ignorant of the scene at the time. Bob talked me into it.

As we pulled up I said, "Let's go in and check out the place. If it seems OK, then I'll come out and get my guitar."

"It's OK. Come on bring your guitar and sign up," Bob said.

"I think I should look around first."

"Fine, Rapson, *I'll* carry your f——g guitar for you!" He said.

"All right, all right. I'll bring it." And up the stairs we went.

I am uncomfortable showing up first for any gathering. How to be fashionably late is still a mystery to me. As usual, we walked into a huge room full of tables, and empty of people. One man, who did not look up as we entered, was walking around arranging chairs. He was the host, Robert Haigh.

Robert had a reputation for a stony demeanor, which he was living up to as he said, "You're early."[10] I felt out of place and out of control, but pretended I knew what was happening. It was like my first time hailing a cab in New York. I kept waving my arm while the cabs passed by. Not sure if I was waving correctly, each unsuccessful hail turned into a hair adjustment maneuver, or a persistently itchy ear. I have since watched many a new performer go through the same emotions. The newcomer anywhere is easy to spot.

My fear was twofold. First, as a former bandleader, I had an inflated opinion of myself; I was afraid my fellow performers would be amateurs, and I would look bad by association. The second, greater, fear was that everyone would be terrific and *I* would appear the amateur.

Either way I was a hyperventilating, self-absorbed wreck by the time my name was called. Fifty people were there to play, and another fifty there to watch. By luck of the draw, I was first. I found out later that Mr. Haigh would put newcomers on early, as he ostensibly drew random names for playing order. Those who showed up every week found themselves playing last.

---

[10] Robert Haigh's friends later assured me that everybody who meets him thinks he hates them. However, he is really a loveable guy who has devoted himself to supporting promising singer songwriters and is remembered in the thank-you section of many a performer's first CD.

"Please welcome, Steve Rapson," he said. The room filled with warm applause. I blindly walked to the stage unprepared to do what I had, a moment before, been certain I was prepared to do. I sat on a stool to play a guitar solo I had played a thousand times before. My left hand was trembling; I could not fret the first chord. Luckily, I did the right thing.

"I'm shaking so much I can't play," I said to the one hundred upturned faces. They applauded and shouted encouragement.

"You can do it!" they called out. I was moved by this heartfelt support. They gave me the courage, if not the skill, to get through the piece. I finished and they cheered (a bit too enthusiastically, I thought) as I walked back to Bob who beamed at his budding protégé.[11]

63
How Does An Opening Act Differ From A Main Act?

Everybody pays to see the main act. Nobody wants to see the opening act. Keep it to twenty minutes and bring as many family and friends as you can.

64
What If I Open For An Inferior Performer?

It may be that the crowd filling the room does not share your opinion of the headliner. Your job is to do the best you can. The club, your manager, and your agent have the task of pairing you with acts you will complement.

---

[11] Bob Fields' ad agency, Commonwealth Creative Associates of Natick, MA, designs my CDs and book covers. Bob continues to encourage me.

65
Should I Take Acting Or Voice Classes?

If you have a natural talent, then improving on it will keep you sharp, so you will be ready when that rare big break comes along.

I am out on the circuit every night. I know all the serious people in the Boston area. Occasionally, I see someone whose act has taken a quantum leap forward from the last time I saw him or her. "Wow! You were great," I say, "What have you been doing?" Without exception, the answer is, "Oh, I've been taking voice lessons." Or, "I've been getting some coaching." Or, "I just returned from six months on the road."

There is nothing like coaching and experience to notch up your act.

66
Will I Always Need Coaching?

Great actors need directors. Great singers take singing lessons. Great speakers hire speechwriters and performance coaches. As you evolve, you want to stay on the path of truth. A coach helps you do that.

67
How Should I Handle Compliments?

Say, "Thank-you, you are very kind." Do not say, "Oh, no! I sucked." Do not launch into a summary of your self-perceived shortcomings. Do not go on about how you could have been much better if only the sound tech knew what he was doing, or the lights were not so bright, if there wasn't so much smoke, or the audience had paid attention. This is self-absorption and narcissism. Everybody recognizes it as such. It is unappealing and people will avoid you if you do not get over it.

68
How Should I Handle Critics?

I suggest you ignore most critics. They will annoy you at the least. Do not casually ask people what they thought of your show. Do not read reviews. Have someone screen them for you. Put the good ones on your wall and burn the bad ones.

There is no such thing as constructive criticism. Indeed, all criticism is destructive. If you see someone coming towards you with the obvious intent of doing you some good, run like hell.

I agree that we need outside opinions of our work; it is the only way to see it as others do. But it is never constructive. Besides, after we are torn down by the casual opinions of others, they do not hang around to help us rebuild. The only critics you should listen to are those who love you, or those you pay. People who receive love or money from you will be truthful and gentle, so as not to interrupt the flow of either.

When I first entered the solo performer scene in Boston, I was a full time speech consultant, and recently retired TV and radio producer. I was insufferably arrogant, and would spontaneously share with other acts what I thought was lacking in their performance. No one hit me. But they should have.

One night, after my own performance, a fellow singer/songwriter returned the favor. He sought me out in the back of the room and told me what was wrong with my act. I did not ask, but he could not contain himself. I stared down the tonsils of this twit going on about my shortfalls, and I did not like it at all. He said I appeared angry on stage, that I was unapproachable. The worst of it was, he was right. It is funny now; and I have since regaled him with my feelings of this big moment between us, of which he has no recollection.

Unless you are compelled to take criticism, avoid it.

Listen to your audience. They are your best critics. They talk with their hands and feet.

69
What About Mikes, Sound Systems, and Lighting?

Here are the basics:

Microphone Technique: For acoustic venues, you will sound much better if you stay a few inches off the mike. The reason rock performers "eat the mike" is to hear themselves over the 100+ decibels of the band, and to avoid feedback.

The mike should be placed just below your mouth, not in front of it. Your mouth is used to smile at the people and to express emotion. You will connect better if they can see all of you. Keep the mike straight up and down and press it to your chin just under your lower lip. This way you will avoid feedback because you are close, the people will see your whole face, and you will sound more natural.

Do not blow into a mike to see if it is on, tap it once instead. Do not say *"testing, testing"* to check the sound. Say a bit of your speech if you are speaking, or sing a few bars if you are singing. If there are any audience members in the room, which there should not be if you are a pro and have shown up early for the sound check, talk to them and tell them what is happening and what is going to happen. Never miss a chance to connect with the people, however unplanned or awkward.

Sound Systems: You need twice as much power as you think you will need. This is not so you will be excessively loud, but to give you head room so that the peaks of your voice and instrument do not distort and annoy your listener's ears. The two most common errors in self-administered sound re-inforcement are improper input trim settings (the knobs that adjust how sensitive each channel input is) and underpowered PA's. In either case, distortion is the result. Sometimes it is subtle, but even subtle distortion is tiring and stressful.

Special Effects: When overused, they cease to be special. A little reverb is all you need. Delay, chorus and flange, hinder more often than help your act.

Lighting: Carry a small portable spotlight with a clamp for those venues that want to put you in a dark corner. Don't forget the long extension cord. Most places have stage lighting so you may never have to use your own.

© 2000 The New Yorker Collection from cartoonbank.com. All Rights Reserved

THE SUDDEN, SURE KNOWLEDGE THAT
ONE'S BEST EFFORTS HAVE COME TO NAUGHT

70
What Happens If I Have An Off Night?

You will have a story to tell. Good stories are about overcoming adversity. Be grateful for the story being delivered to you. One off night, or one great night, is not a big deal. If you have many off nights, you might reconsider your material, your delivery, or your audience, in that order.

A friend of mine played in the NFL. He was a defensive back for the New York Giants. He is highly intelligent, handsome, and articulate. After football he went into financial sales and became a motivational speaker, pointing out the similarities between selling and chasing wide receivers. At the beginning of every speech, he held up a short strip of 16mm film and said:

"I played in the NFL for ten years, so I thought we'd start out by looking at my highlight film."

It was a great opening that always worked: quick, visual, and self-deprecating. His football stories were fascinating, although the tie-in to selling was less dependable. He was refining his material when a big computer company hired him as the keynote speaker for their annual sales meeting. Most of his speeches had been in small rooms to a dozen people. Now he was in the big time, with five hundred high-powered sales types to enthrall. He was apprehensive, but not one to back down from a challenge.

Here he is, ladies and gentlemen, Mr. Football! Mr. Success! Mr Motivation!

I was back stage when he died. He had started strong, but when the laughs stopped coming, his words echoed over a deathly silent crowd. After many painful minutes, a drunken salesman climbed onto a table and encouraged everyone to join him in a company cheer.

He told me later, "Steve, when that guy staggered up and started yelling, I knew it was over. I got real hot, and was ready to take a running leap from the stage and go table to table. I'd take him out with a high forearm to the head, continue across the tables, out the back door, and into the bar. Eight to ten seconds, tops. Instead, I just wrapped it up. I think the applause was for my fast close."

Today, my friend is a senior VP with a big company. He appears as a company spokesman on TV. He has a good story to tell.

71
How Can I Keep My Act Fresh?

Jack Falvey[12] has been giving the same speech for years. "You never get tired of hitting them over the fence, of seeing just how far it will go this time!" says Jack.

Jack's keynote speech, *How the Best Get Better In Selling,* always begins with a tennis lesson. He gets the audience on their feet holding a make-believe tennis racquet in front of them and bouncing up and down on their toes. The energy level in the room is off the charts. Then he asks, "Are we really learning to play tennis?" He waits for an answer. *What is preventing you from really learning tennis, since everything I told you was accurate?* The audience is now involved, shouting out their answers. He makes the point that everything he will tell them about selling is true, but you have to be in front of a real customer to get good at it. I have seen Jack do this many times. Like a hearing virtuoso musician play a well-known piece, you know every note, but it is a pleasure to hear the performance unfold yet again.

If you do get tired of succeeding with your well-crafted act, then it is time for a vacation, not a new act. What *does* get old is material that does not deliver.

72
Should I Change My Act For Different Audiences?

It takes so long to get sixty minutes of material to work consistently that it might be easier to find the right audience for your act, than to find different material. Thankfully audiences do not vary that much. The only

---

[12] Jack Falvey is an internationally known keynote speaker, management consultant, author of several books on careers, sales, and sales management and a frequent contributor to the Manager's Journal column of the *Wall Street Journal.* www.falvey.org.

caveats: babies or alcohol. If either is present, you are in trouble. Both tend to become the center of attention, no matter how good your act.

In the comedy world, there is the curse and blessing of national TV exposure. Once you do your best ten minutes on TV, you have to retire that painstakingly crafted material. This is because comics, unlike singers and public speakers, are expected to have new material when they come through town again. Singers, on the other hand, are expected to do the same song over and over until they die.

73
What If The Audience Doesn't Like Me?

It is most probably because you do not like them, or you are afraid of them. Collectively, audiences are smart. They detect the slightest off-tones in demeanor, like a dog that smells fear. Have you ever felt embarrassed for a performer? Audiences do not like feeling that way.

The quickest way to resolve this is to stop thinking about what they think of you. Develop a thick skin. When you are doing your act, get out of yourself for a half-hour. Give them what they want. Then you will get what you want. You cannot reverse it. Would you promise a stove some wood just as soon at it gives you some heat?

Tell them you appreciate that they are there, that they are listening. Do this in thought, word, and deed. You cannot phone it in. How many times have you heard a speaker/performer say, "It's a pleasure to be here..." without the slightest note of pleasure in their voice, on their face, in their body language?

Love them. Let them know you love them. They will love you. I guarantee it.

74
How Should I Talk To The Audience?

Talk up to them. Jack Benny, when asked the secret to his success, said, "I don't know for sure, but the one thing I always did was assume they were smarter than I was and go from there." How many successful singers, comics, or speakers do you know that have made a career of insulting their audience?

It is better to be like Jack Benny and assume they are smarter than you are. Create an image of your audience as a collection of Nobel Prize winners. If you are giving a talk on redesigning computers, imagine Bill Gates, Ken Olsen, and Ed DeCastro in the front row. Talk up.

75
What If Somebody Wants An Autograph?

Give it to them with a smile and a thank-you. Before you go to bed that night, thank someone more important than you for your good fortune and ask for the power to remain humble.

76
Are There Alternative Venues?

The streets work well. You do not have to ask permission, although you may need a street performer's license. The acoustics are always good and your stage is right there. Of course some municipalities will want to move you along, arrest you, or get you to stop. You move on and set up shop elsewhere. A good friend of mine is a major market TV news anchor. I met him on the streets twenty-five years ago. He was a mime/juggler/actor. He made several hundred dollars a week with his street act. It was a big decision for him to quit the streets and go into TV. He started at the bottom and now is near the top. Many internationally known acts started on the street.[13]

---

[13] A friend who works the streets said a guy tossed a quarter in his guitar case saying, "Shut the f--- up."

"Sir, *shut the f--- up* is a dollar," I suggested as a reply for the next time. It is rare for a street performer to suffer verbal abuse. It can happen, though, and that which doesn't kill you, will indeed make you stronger.

For example, guitarist Stanley Jordan and singer/songwriters Tracy Chapman and Martin Sexton. My experience is that the streets, or open mikes, are good places to take stock of your act. If you aren't connecting, then you know something has to change. If you are connecting, your guitar case will fill quickly.

Consider entertaining at nursing homes, where you will be paid reasonably. There is a circuit for acts aimed at schools—junior and senior high and college. They have annual conventions where the people who hire acts meet. You could volunteer your talent to support worthy causes. It beats a bar gig in appreciation, and you build your mailing list.

I volunteered to entertain children at the Shriner's Burn Center in Boston. A dozen children and teens, horribly burned and disfigured, walked and wheeled into a room where I was set up. I was stricken with fear that my act was insufficient to reach those whose suffering I could not begin to fathom. However, they soon showed me they were just kids, ready to be diverted for a while, ready to laugh, and we did, together.

My grandfather, Cecil Rapson, was a part-time street preacher. He had an old, round-shouldered bus that he drove to downtown Boston each Sunday. He stood outside the bus on a box. A soapbox, I think. He was always smiling, calling gently to passers-by. He told them Sunday services were about to begin in the bus. After attracting his flock, he stood in the aisle and preached his message of the week. No church required. You want to preach? Start preaching.

77
What If The Audience Wants Something Different?

He who pays the piper calls the tune. That is why performers of all kinds make so little money in the beginning. If you don't want to play what people are asking for—and they are not usually asking to hear your material—then you will not be paid very much, if anything.

You must decide what you can afford to do. Is it cover gigs, where you do hits of the day for decent pay? Or original gigs where you do what you have written, and for which you may be poorly paid? You will probably start with covers, mix in the originals, and the marketplace will decide your reward.

hould I Act On TV or Radio?

Learn to talk normally in an artificial situation. Learn to speak prepared material as if it were not prepared. Learn to deliver stories the same way every time—as if it were the first time. The media demands these skills.

Listen to the shows you want to get on so you will be familiar with their format. After you call to find out the procedure for pitching them, send your press kit. If you are scheduled for an interview, send them a list of suggested questions. Most interviewers appreciate this and will use some or all of them. A professional interviewer will re-phrase them and slip them in seamlessly.

You send the list of questions because you know the good answers. You have prepared and rehearsed your anecdotes, stories, and factoids. An appropriate question allows you to launch into each one. When you do this, you identify yourself as a professional entertainer. If an interviewer ever discounts this advance work on your part, as one did to me, you can be sure you are dealing with an amateur. You will need to be doubly prepared and on your toes.

Your stories should be thirty seconds or less. What you want is a nice back and forth between you and the interviewer. This will happen if you are both prepared. There will be plenty of spontaneity. It is much easier to be spontaneous when neither of you is worried about how dull the interview is.

On TV you will have even less time. You must be tighter with your stories and anecdotes, nothing over fifteen seconds. You cannot refer to notes, so you will have to have everything memorized. You will be visible, so your clothing and make-up needs to be thought about in advance. If you are going to perform, you need to think about blocking; i.e. Will you be moving about? Where will your guitar be? Your capo? Your cord? Your water? Your set list?

The most effective people on TV and radio are those that have mastered the art of being a phony. In the best sense.

79
How Do To I Get Audience Participation?

Once or twice you may want the audience to sing along or respond aloud to your questions. In regard to the latter, do not ask a question of any kind unless you want a response. For example, you might step up to the mike and ask, "How's everybody doing?" Many performers do this. I always respond with, "Great, thanks." Some performers look surprised and confused, as if they are being heckled. If you ask a question be prepared for an answer.

If you want the audience to sing along, tell them exactly what you want. Show them how to sing it, and keep after them till they do. Never be satisfied with half efforts. Encourage them to give it up. When they do, never make fun of them. It is all good.

Above all, keep it simple. If your sing-along is a complex lyric of many words, you will be sorely disappointed.

80
What Should I Wear On Stage?

What you wear is part of your stage persona. It should send the same message you and your material send. Beginning performers are uncomfortable with clothing that makes them stick out. Since you have to be comfortable to perform, wear what feels right to you. As you develop your act, you can introduce more flamboyant clothes.

Want to make a statement quickly? Wear a hat. Are you physically fit and attractive? Show it off. Need some bits of business? (Things you do that appear not to be part of the main act, but, of course, really are.) You could wear layers of lightweight clothing and remove various articles throughout the show. Les Brown, America's #1 motivational speaker, strides on stage, removes his jacket and hangs it on a chair. It builds expectation and positive tension. Since I saw Les, I do it all the time.

Consider your wardrobe. Make it part of your act.

81
What Should I Do
Before My Performance?

If it is appropriate, mingle with the people before the show. Meet as many as you can. Learn their names and ask questions. Listen. When you go on, you are no longer a stranger, you are a friend. You are pre-sold.

Just before you go on, retire to a quiet place. Take three deep breaths each followed by a long slow exhale. This will thoroughly relax your body. Your mind will follow. Think about the people you love and who love you. Think about the immensity of the universe and the specks of dust that our planet and we are. Ask for the power to see the truth and to touch others with what you see. Imagine yourself with those you feel most relaxed and happy. This prepares you to be you at your best.

82
What Should I Do
After My Performance?

Say thank-you. Smile. Bow. Exit. Few performers in the lower ranks bow at the end of their performance. At the top, everybody bows. It does not have to be a big production. Make it simple, quick and deliberate. Step to the left or right. Pause. Bend at the waist. Pause. Straighten up and exit before they stop clapping. You do not want to be bowing in silence. The depth of your bow is up to you. [14]

---

[14] Bowing is serious business in Japan. The Japanese bow at any provocation. Subordinates bow to superiors who bow in return. Bowing etiquette dictates that your bow must be a speck lower than your superior's bow. If your superior likes you he, and it is usually he in Japan, will bow slightly so that you, too, must bow just a little. If the boss is doing a power play number on your head, he will bow to you deeply and long, thus forcing you to grovel even lower than he. You have to sneak a look up to check the depth of your bow against that of your ever so humble superior.

After you leave the stage, mingle with the people. Thank them for coming. Listen more than you speak. Get somebody else to tear you away from your people. Make it easy for people to sign your mailing list, buy your stuff, and meet you. Further bowing is optional.

83
What Is The First Thing
I Should Say To My Audience?

The moment the audience sees you, you are on. They notice your carriage as you walk to the stage, where you look, who you look at, the expression on your face. They judge the ease, or lack thereof, with which you strap on your guitar, arrange yourself at the piano, in front of the mike. Before you do a thing, you begin to establish your rapport with the audience.

Your body language should communicate ease and command. When you walk to the stage, keep your head up, shoulders back. Look to your left and right and acknowledge others with eye contact and a smile.

At the mike, look around. Look into the eyes of as many people as you can. Smile. Before speaking, take care of technical chores like mikes and cords. Keep your hands away from your face and hair. If you feel nervous, be "dead from the neck down" when you speak or sing. This is because gestures and body movements are most effective when planned and rehearsed.

A half-minute may have passed from your introduction to your first words. Yet, without a word, you have communicated clearly to the audience that, *"I am happy to be here, and am eagerly anticipating my performance for you. I am confident, having done this successfully many times before. I like you all, and am sure you like me."*

Direct your first words to the audience. Private banter with staff or sound people does not draw people in. Say a quick thank-you to your host, then sing your song. If you talk to the audience you become a public speaker. Here the rules for effective public speaking:

Be Prepared. What you say must be written intelligently, edited mercilessly, and rehearsed endlessly. Use biographical snippets, social commentary, song intros, and anecdotes from the spectacularly interesting life you are leading.

Be Interesting. Amazing facts known only to you, or juicy gossip about your life are good.

Be Done. If you cannot be interesting at least have the decency to be brief.

Your song writing will benefit from this same formula. Condense your ideas so they are thought provoking and dense with meaning, the way poetry and verse are meant to be. If your song is short and people love it, they'll call for encores:

"Tell us more, oh musical bard! Please wax poetic further as we attend your every word, however brief."

However, if the people *do not* like your short song, you are done soon enough, for which they will bless you, and maybe give you another shot. Heads you win, tails you win.

There is no downside to brevity in artistic expression. The best way to be brief is to prepare. Prepare everything, from the first hello to the last good-bye.

84
What Is The Last Thing
I Should Say To My Audience?

Thank-You. You have been a wonderful audience. You have made this night for me. You, You, You. Get in the habit of using the you word.

© 2000 The New Yorker Collection from cartoonbank.com. All Rights Reserved

"Me, me, me me me me ME!"

85
How Do I Overcome Stage Fright?

The cure for stage fright is practice. In addition, Ron Harding, teacher, author, and advertising consultant, offers the following.

The Twin Fears:
Fear of Failure, Fear of Rejection
by Ron Harding

In a study done in 1973 by R.H. Bruskin Associates, the number one fear was speaking in public. That fear even outranked fear of dying! Experts who have studied performance fear divide it into two categories, Situation Anxiety and Trait Anxiety.

SITUATION ANXIETY: These fears are focused on a particular appearance. What leads to anxiety here is a sense of being in a strange place, not being prepared, lack of familiarity with the room or equipment, any number of variables that can lead to a misstep. Situation anxiety is based on a loss of control. This fear is usually internalized by the sentence, "God, I hope I don't make a fool of myself." Here are some tips to help you minimize situational fear.

Prepare and practice: Get your performance down pat beforehand. This leads to a sense of internal flow. Practice performing in front of a group of friends, relatives, and for free to take the edge off. Repetition builds familiarity and confidence. Having some prepared off the cuff remarks to get you into the flow of things helps put you and the audience at ease.

Warm-up: Get to the place where you are to perform early. Check the equipment, check the lights, and check any distractions that may work against you and eliminate as many as you can before the audience arrives. Talk to anybody in the place. Get the juices flowing. Talk to those who are first to arrive. Make them feel at home.

Practice deep breathing: When people are nervous they tend to take shallow breaths. Decreasing oxygen makes you light headed, jittery, clammy. Breathing deeply tells your body, everything is OK.

Use an introduction that relaxes you and your audience. Write your introduction out for whoever is going to introduce you. Make it short. Cite your achievements. Let the audience relax, by letting them know you know what you are doing.

Concentrate: Communicate your message. What you have to say, sing, or show is what is important. Forget about you. The more you disappear into your material, the stronger your impact, believability, and acceptance.

TRAIT ANXIETY: These fears are learned in childhood. They can be summarized as the feeling that *"if people really knew me..."* Trait anxiety is what leads to dependence on alcohol, drugs, abusive relationships, et al. It stems from feelings of unworthiness, no genuine self-esteem: those tapes put in our heads by well meaning parents, teachers, and authority figures. Become successful enough and a good psychiatrist will help you sort it all out. Until then, here are some cheaper ways to deal with trait anxiety.

Positive imaging: See yourself doing a good job in advance. Imagine the applause. In that screening room in your head, rehearse your success. Famous athletes, comics, motivational speakers all prime themselves before an event. They see themselves emerge in triumph.

Modeling: Emulate someone in your field you respect and admire. Become them! Johnny Carson pretended to be his idol, Jack Benny. Jack Benny pretended to be *his* idol, Frank Fay. Robin Williams imitated Jonathan Winters. Bob Guccione imitated Hugh Hefner. Nothing succeeds like success. Copy it!

Have a beginning, middle, and end: All public entertainment works on the cycle of threes. Plays have three acts. Comics set up the gag, repeat it, and pay it off. Greek playwrights discovered this principle three thousand years ago and everybody who ignores it is probably out of work. Start your speech, or gig by telling the audience who you are and what they are going to see. Then build on that. Focus your material. Keep it building, in energy and excitement! Plant some sure-fire gags, observations, and numbers that you can depend on to work. Then wrap it up! Have a big finish. Then... get off

Work the room with eye contact: In every audience there are people who laugh first and applaud loudest. Play to them. Let the rest of the audience catch up. Look at people. Smile, nod. Let them in on the act. People come to every event wanting to have a good time. Invite them in throughout the performance.

End with positive reinforcement: Thank the audience for coming. Thank them for being attentive, intelligent, attractive, whatever good side they have shown while they were with you. Invite them back. To the place. To you. You want to feel good about you. Your audience wants to feel appreciated, too. Make a personal connection and your anxieties will not hold you back.

Ron Harding is a master of the extemporaneous speech. He is relaxed and casual as he instructs and amuses his audience. He gives no hint of the years of practice and study that allow him to pull a well-crafted anecdote magically out of his hat. Ron, like all artists, makes it looks easy.

When my partner, Maureen Keiller, and I opened for Don White, we were blessed with an ideal performing environment: A full house, dimmed room, a well-lit stage, an attentive audience facing in our direction, laughing in the right spots, singing along where they should. Although there was nothing to fear, halfway through I lost my concentration. This is an early symptom of stage fright. It is a clue to buckle down and pay attention to what you are doing. It feels like a spirit is haunting you, looking for a way in. We were singing a song I knew well, having written it, and I shifted to automatic. This left my front brain free to muse about where I was, how I was doing, who was listening, and, the fatal trigger: *What they thought about it.* I was going to lose it.

I closed my eyes and let the spirit of fear pass through me, over me, around me and off to wherever spirits go when they do not find a home in your head. At the same time, I concentrated on what I was supposed to be thinking about. *G in the bass, second string first fret... third finger, two-three-four now. A Little Bit a Crow...*It was not perfect. But nobody knew. Not even the lovely Maureen who usually keeps a mental list of these things for post-performance review.

Stage fright is also a symptom of perfectionism and self-absorption, an ego out of control. These character defects can be minimized with prayer, fasting, clean living, and practice.

86
What Should I Do If I Blank Out?

Fake it. When the fear gets into your head, or you lose concentration and draw a blank, fake it. If you do not give a visual clue that a mistake has occurred no one will notice. No matter how obvious and gross you think it was, no one will notice.

Have you ever seen a performer grimace, roll their eyes, or smile in an embarrassed way at a mistake? Often they say, "I'm sorry." This is the only clue an audience has that you are not happy with your performance. Do not give them this clue.

Jazz guitarist Howard Roberts said when he plays an obvious 'clam' (a bad note) he repeats it several times, intimating that he intended to play it all along.

I was the bandleader for a good friend's wedding. During the Father/Daughter Dance I was singing *Where are you going my little one, little one...* I drew a blank on the rest of the song. To not diminish the moment, I faked it by improvising a "joy of family, circle of life," monologue, while the band carried on. Nobody knew but my drummer, a pick-up guy from Berklee, who complimented me on the smooth cover.

If you are totally at a loss of what to do next, pause; take a drink of water. Engage in banter with someone in the front row, "So, where are you guys from?" "How's everybody doing, OK?" You could say and do nothing while you collect your thoughts. This is called 'commanding the silence'. It is a powerful technique that requires practice and courage to pull off. When you are silent, you build tension in the room. The audience will become quiet, too. The longer you are silent, the more tension builds. Whatever you say or do next will be of high impact. You could say, "Boo!" or just clear your throat, and get a big response. If you have lost it, at the end of the silence, say so. Everything will be fine.

87
Can I Bring Notes With Me On Stage?

If you are an academic giving a technical speech, notes are more than acceptable: they lend credence to your presentation.

If you are singing a song from your heart, reading the lyrics will not seem quite right to the audience. I see this at open mikes frequently. I have done it myself. "I just finished my new song and I can't wait till I actually know it before I perform it for you." This is not usually effective and you don't even get a good read on how the audience like your new song because you screwed it up. Now I never do it. Even at Open Mikes I wait until a new song is fully ready before attempting it. Jimmy Tingle read some new material at Club Passim, perhaps destined for his 60 Minutes II spot on national TV. It worked for him.

Mortimer Adler in his book, *How to Speak, How to Listen,* suggests using index cards with the main points of your speech in order on each card. This keeps you on track, but allows you to speak more extemporaneously.

88
What If There Is Too Much Noise?

Ignore it and continue with your act. If it is a jet plane going over, you could pause until it passes. If it is a particularly noisy table, play to the quiet table. If it is a bar and everyone is ignoring you, look at one person. Play to them. If they turn away, find someone else. The temptation in these situations is to turn inward and protect yourself by noticing nothing and no one. If you wish to grow as a performer, you cannot do this. You must use every opportunity to connect with the people.

I was playing at a coffeeshop when a table of loud teenagers began talking over me. I ended abruptly. "Thank-you very much!" I said, packing up. Few people knew I was annoyed. Even the talkers called for more. But I was done. They got into my head and that was that.

We sometimes think, as the crowd drowns us out, *"If I were good enough, they would pay attention."* Alternatively, we may think, *"These people are inconsiderate jerks."* It is *"I suck."* or *"They suck."* Not usually true, and cancerous to think either way. With the right mind-set I could have played to the people who were listening.

Eventually you can be discriminating about where you work. Until then, mental serenity through the storm is the most you can hope for.

89
Should I Move Around Or Stand Still?

Unless you are moving because the spirit moves you, be still. Unless you are using gestures that you have carefully rehearsed to support your material, be still.

90
Do Gestures Help, Or Distract?

If they are natural, they add to your performance. If they are contrived, they detract. If you are nervous, gestures will look nervous. Touching your face and hair, for example, makes you look unsure. Fondling the microphone cord looks nervous. Walking back and forth with no apparent motivation is a sign of something not right within. This is what people do when they are not comfortable.

On the *Today Show,* Katie Couric interviewed a Coast Guard Commander about search and recovery efforts off Nantucket. An Egyptian Airliner had gone down. The Commander was in uniform, nicely grayed and commanderly. His office was well-lit, he was shot from mid-waist, and positioned in a three-quarter stance to the camera so that his head was turned slightly left. This is more flattering than a head on shot, but beginners, like the Commander, look posed. Professionals. like Stone Phillips, appear natural doing this. In addition, the Commander had been coached to stay still as he answered Katie's questions. Therefore, when he gave a semi-repressed shrug, it stuck out because he was not moving otherwise. He communicated his unfamiliarity with a TV interview, and his discomfort, despite his effort to hide both. When your body language is off people notice.

When stand-up news people do live remotes their heads bob around and eyebrows dance as they talk, but everything from the neck down is rock-still. It is hard enough getting the words right in thirty seconds, without a stray twitch sending an unintended message. This is what the Coast Guard commander was instructed to do. However, he did not have the experience to fully execute it.

Being still is analogous to keeping your mouth shut in an unfamiliar situation. It solves the problem of inappropriate or inadvertent communication via gestures and movements. It is also a good way to hide how you feel, especially when you do not want people to know how you feel. It is boring. At the beginner level, it is what novice politicians and business people are trained to do.

The next level is to be yourself at your best. Preparation and practice will help you feel less anxious. Deep breathing will relax you. If you feel normal, you will move normally. This is best strategy for most of us.

At the top level, plan and rehearse your movements and gestures. Comedian Jack Benny put his hand to his face along with a wide-eyed take to the audience. That gesture became his trademark. He did it whenever he wanted to let the audience in on the gag and get a laugh. For example, a mugger approaches Benny with a gun, "Your money or your life!" he shouts. Since Benny's stage persona is that of a tightwad, he does the hand to the face thing (chin in palm, fingers drumming on the cheek) and gets a big laugh.

"C'mon, your money or your life!" says the impatient thief.

"I'm thinking." Benny says.

When comics impersonated Jack Benny, the first thing they did was assume the hand-to-face pose.

Jackie Gleason was a master of non-verbal communication. In 1948, still an unknown working in Las Vegas, he shared a bill with Chas Chase, an old vaudevillian. Chas walked out in a tuxedo, smoking a cigarette. He ate the cigarette. Then he ate his suit.[15] First his cuffs, then his sleeves, and so on, as elegant music played in the background. He said not a word during this non-verbal tour de force. Gleason discovered that if he walked out and watched Chas eat his suit, the audience would go nuts. Gleason looked on in mock horror getting laughs with his eye rolls and double takes.

Lily Tomlin, in a film documentary, prepares for her show, *The Search for Signs of Intelligent Life in the Universe*. There is a scene with her performance coach where she has her arms above her head, rocking back and forth as she says her lines. The coach interrupts:

"That won't work, you have to hit this word and then lift your arms," she said.

"I know, I know. It's new words with new movements. Give me a minute... the computer is still processing," said Lily.

That little exchange tells the whole story about what it takes to incorporate words and movements into a professional performance that eventually looks like it is being invented on the spot.

In another documentary jazz legend Ella Fitzgerald is rehearsing with her little band. They are doing *How High the Moon*. Ella is saying, "OK, now, when we come out of the second chorus, I'll take three steps right. On the downbeat to the sax solo, Bill (drummer), you give me a big hit in the high hat, and I'll dip like I'm on a string, turn around and come back. I'll look at you..."

---

[15] His suit was presumably fashioned from some flimsy, edible substance. I believe the cigarette was real.

Pros make it look easy and natural. It is neither. When it works the audience and you both have a great time.

91
How Come Everybody Doesn't Recognize My Greatness?

It *is* annoying, isn't it?

92
What Happens If I Run Out Of Time?

Do you know how long your material takes? Each song, each anecdote and story? This is the *be prepared* part of the business. A little known secret of the stage is a collorary to the "leave them laughing" rule. When you are in the final third or even the last half of your act and something you do has blown the roof off the room, then close on it. End it right there. Say thanks, bow, and leave immediately. It is the best thing a performer can do. Get in the habit of closing on a big response, even if you have not done what you consider your best material. Only good things can happen.

First, you left them laughing or at least shouting approval. Second, you closed on a high note, a big climax, however serendipitous. Third, you have left them wanting more which is another show biz maxim. Fourth, you have time for an encore, which is likely to be requested, and you still have some great material left.

Beginners are often out of touch with the audience; they miss opportunities to close strong. Rather than applause at show's end, there are shuffling feet and chairs scraping on the floor as people decide for themselves when it is over. Keep it short, finish strong, and you will rise very quickly.

Do as I say, not as I do. I was in New Hampshire to play an open mike in a church hall. I had three new songs I was anxious to try out. My first song was a solo guitar rendition of John Phillip Sousa's *The Stars and Stripes Forever* from my CD, *Patriotic Guitar*. I nailed it and the crowd went wild. They stomped, shouted, and clapped thunderously. I had never received such an enthusiastic ovation, and I ate it up. Do you think I did the right thing? Of course not. I forgot that I should have stood up right then, bowed, said thanks and left immediately. Instead, I launched into another song. It was OK, although the same heights were not achieved. Now I play that song last.

If you get a strong response, close and do not be greedy for more.

93
Should I Accept Requests?

Requests are a two-edge sword. You like the attention, but unless they request something from your repertoire, you will disappoint them. A good show has a carefully programmed flow. Requests can be a monkey wrench thrown into the gears. If there are a hundred people in the room and one person makes a request, you work for that one person. Again, not in your best interest or the crowd's.

Stick with your act. Deflect requests with a smile, and say you will do something even better.

94
How Do I Know When To Do An Encore?

There should be an element of compulsion for you to return to the stage. If you are too eager, it will show. The people will ask you to return by continuous applause and shouts of, "More," until you return. Or until someone comes to the stage and says, "Ladies and gentlemen, (*Insert your name here*), has left the building."

95
How Do I Do An Encore?

Return to the stage, presuming you left. Begin the next song. Do not—I repeat, do not—launch into an extended speech. You were called back to do more of what you do. If it is not speaking, do not speak, unless your act has The Highly Entertaining Encore Bit.

96
Should I Accept Tips?

Yes, with grace and gratitude.

© 2000 The New Yorker Collection from cartoonbank.com. All Rights Reserved

"At the conclusion of this evening's concert, ladies and gentlemen, I 'll thank you for not forgetting the tip jar."

97
How Do I Tastefully Pass The Hat'?

Get somebody else to do it for you. Share the proceeds with them. If you are in a room where the audience comes and goes, pass the hat a few times. Pass it after two or three songs. Do whatever you feel you can comfortably do. It is your payday. If you leave a jar in front of you, or near the door, you will get much less.

98
How Do I Handle Hecklers?

Speakers, comedians, and musicians have their own methods. The clichéd retort, "I remember when I had my first beer..." is not always effective. If you turn on an audience member, you may lose everyone else. Here are techniques that work.

Guitarist Andre Segovia used a classic technique. When people were talking or coughing during his performance, he stopped playing, removed a handkerchief from his pocket and discreetly coughed into it. He then returned to a playing position but did not play until it was quiet. This will work best when you are a legend in your own time.

You could do one or more of the following when a heckler shouts out something, or people are talking too loud.

Method 1. Stop and turn to the offender, say nothing for a few seconds, then return to your act. This will usually get a laugh, which shifts the burden to the heckler. They may not respond further.

Method 2. If Method 1 was insufficient, stop and say, "I'm sorry...?" in a matter of fact way, leaning forward as if you did not quite catch it. No matter what is said, next ask the person's name, where they are from, etc. End with, "OK. Well, nice talking with you." Then go back to your act. Most people are uncomfortable with this kind of attention being drawn to them, and they will quiet down.

Method 3. If they continue even after Method 2, leave the stage. Go sit with the heckler, or walk as close to them as you can. Bring your mike if possible. Engage them, be friendly and non-aggressive. I was being destroyed at a drinker's paradise a few years ago. Nothing worked, so I stopped playing and walked over and sat with the people. *Was there any way I could get a break?* I was light and friendly; they were drunk. After a few minutes of raucous banter, I said I had get back to playing. One of them said, "You're all right, Steve. Your music sucks, but you're OK"

Method 4. Ignore the heckler completely. This works well if you have a good rapport with the rest of the crowd, and your material is going over. You just keep doing your act as if the heckler is not there. Quite often the people sitting with the heckler, or the immediate crowd, will shush them for you.

I was working an up-scale hotel lounge recently. One table was filled with partiers. After my first song, an aggressive older woman at that table snapped her fingers at me.

"Hey! Let's pick it up," she said. My artist's soul cringed at this shabby treatment. Several potential retorts flashed on my computer screen, like Schwartzenegger's killer robot in *The Terminator.*

I selected one. "I'm the guy with the guitar, baby. Get used to it."

In feeble defense of my behavior, I *did* say this light-heartedly with a smile. The table erupted with laughter. The woman, flushed with embarrassment, mumbled and turned away. I handled the heckler, but did not win a fan.

Later, at another table, a couple was obviously enjoying my show. I sang right to them. They responded with smiles and applause. At the break I sat with them. We bonded immediately. They were from Vancouver, and invited me to stay with them when I gig there. I gave them one of my CDs, and we exchanged cards, parting with the promise of staying in touch.

I behave myself when treated well. However, as a professional entertainer it is my job make them like me, not the reverse. If I had been nicer to the rude woman, I might have made a fan and sold a few CDs, rather than giving them away. Our first instinct is to poke back when we are poked. If we want to succeed as performers, however, we must give people a couple of chances.

When you are heckled, try to suppress your survival instincts, and cultivate your friendly nature. At least you are being noticed.

99
What If They Are Not Listening Me?

Listen to them, which is hard to do if you are thinking about how they are not listening to you.

I have learned a few tricks to get their attention. One is to *set yourself on fire*. This is means a high-energy attention-grabbing bit to start your show. Alternatively, you could become very quiet. Play and sing increasingly softer. Speak quietly and intimately. It amazes me how a noisy room will come down with you. Whether they will stay with you depends on what they hear when it gets quiet. This is where your material must deliver.

Above all, you must be focused on what you are about. If you are, you will be less likely to notice what is going on in the audience. The Russian actor Konstantin Stanislavsky (1863-1938) came to the same conclusion:

> *I began to understand that I felt so pleasant and comfortable on the stage because my public exercises centered my attention on the perceptions and states of my body, at the same time drawing my attention away from what was happening on the other side of the footlights, in the auditorium beyond the black and terrible hole of the proscenium arch. In what I was doing I ceased to be afraid of the audience, and at times forgot that I was on the stage. I noticed that it was especially at such times that my creative mood was most pleasant.*
>
> *...The more the actor wishes to amuse his audience, the more the audience will sit in comfort waiting to be amused, and not even trying to play its part in the play on the stage before them. But as soon as the actor stops being so concerned with his audience, the latter begins to watch the actor.*

In the same way, we find children and animals innately attractive. They are not self-aware; they just do what they do, unconcerned about who may be watching.

In the advertising world there is a maxim that says: When in doubt, put the product next to babies or puppies and film the result. The naturalness and authenticity of innocents is appealing. We are most appealing as performers when we are focussed on our act and become, for the moment, innocents ourselves.

© 2000 The New Yorker Collection from cartoonbank.com. All Rights Reserved

"Thank you. You've been a great audience."

Have you noticed when a friend or relative gets carried away telling a story—one they care about and re-live as they tell it—how their face becomes animated? How they gesticulate enthusiastically, and their voice modulates up and down? Don't you find them highly appealing at those moments? Audiences want the truth. They feel they are getting it when a performer is immersed in his act.

Stanislavsky's observation suggests that to be most effective—happiest—we must act without thought or attachment to outcome. Thinkers in several cultures have put forth this idea over the centuries. Epictetus, the Greek Stoic philosopher of the first century AD made this observation about desiring certain outcomes:

> *...It matters not what the outward thing may be; to set store by it is to place thyself in subjection to it. Where is the difference between crying, "Woe is me I know not what to do, bound hand and foot as I am to my books so that I cannot stir!" and crying, "Woe is me, I have not time to read!" As though a*

book were not as much an outward thing, and independent of the will, as office and power and the receptions of the great.

Japanese martial artists use a concept called, *Mu shin no shin* meaning mind of no mind. Derived from Buddhism, it means a warrior must attack or defend without thought. If the possibility of victory or defeat creeps into the mind before acting, then the warrior most likely will fail.

In Chinese Zen Buddhism is the *Parable of the Water Buffalo:*

A water buffalo passes though a small window
Its head, its horns, finally its hooves,
All of the great beast emerges
Only its tail does not.

The master explains that in pursuing our ideal we almost get there, but then we think of the impossibility of the task, and, in the thinking, defeat ourselves.

This wisdom from other lands and other times is paraphrased in New Age self-help language as, *To be successful, focus on process not outcome. Life is a journey not a destination.* These may seem like shallow cliches to those who have heard them too many times in the face of difficult personal obstacles. However, when we see the ancient underpinnings of these ideas, they take on more substance and ring true to those of us looking for the path to success as performers.

100
Is All This Necessary?

Humans, like animals, will naturally take the path of least resistance. Although the lion has to run to catch the antelope, she is not going to run faster than required to do so. It is our human nature to do what is required, and no more, to get what we want. If we do less than what is required, we will not get what we want.

Some performers walk on stage one day, open their mouths, and are embraced by the adoring masses. Is this you? Others work for years and seem to stay in the same place. We hope this is not you. Most of us are on the Great Middle Path. We must work harder than we would if we had a choice.

The 80/20 rule states that twenty percent of your effort produces eighty percent of your results. Where are your results, however meager, coming from? Do more of that. This is easier than identifying what you are doing wrong and trying to fix it. Fixing is hard. Changing is hard. This is not to say that repair and revision are not necessary, but look to the good first. You may never have to change the not so good if you get what you want by doing what already works. If nothing is working, then do something else.

It is important to distinguish between twenty years' experience and one year's experience twenty times. As Les Brown says, "If you want to keep on getting what you're getting, then keep on doing what you're doing."

101
What Is The Meaning Of Life?

I thought you would never ask.

What Gore Vidal Said

When you finally know the truth
Of life and love and all that stuff,
Along will come some callow youth
Who thinks to call your bluff.
Speak little, if at all,
Lest your wisdom be purloined.
Pray, be like Gore Vidal,
Who cryptically enjoined:
"The meaning of life?
Why, yes, I know. It's true.
I won it fair through stress and strife
And see no reason to share it now with you."

Steve Rapson

Life has no meaning; you bring meaning to it.

Joseph Campbell

PUBLIC SPEAKING

1
How Do I Become An Inspiring Speaker?

Be inspired. Great speakers are possessed by something larger than themselves. They are zealots and missionaries in their devotion to their idea or cause.

Avoid the temptation to adopt the style of inspiring speakers you have seen. They are inspiring because of what possessed them. Their voices rise and fall with that inner motivation. Their body language is a natural symptom of the fire within. Build your own inner fire and you will move and speak in your own inspiring way. You cannot fake it because you will not know what that way is until you are inspired.

You are inspiring when you wear your heart on your sleeve. Your audience will be inspired when they see in you the god-like quality they, too, could possess when they surrender to a larger ideal, just as you have.

People are inspired by visions of their own greatness. An inspiring speaker allows us to see the path we could take to get there. It is the same for inspiring preachers or inspiring algebra teachers.

2
How Long Does It Take To
Write A Good Speech?

Professional writers produce a thousand words a day. This is four minutes of talking. A twenty-minute speech might take you five days to write and re-write. After writing comes practice. Winston Churchill suggested you practice one hour for each minute of speech. Add another three days. Your research might be your lifetime of experience, or a few hours in the library. Research is the *x factor*.

If you are a world authority on your topic, if you are a professional writer, if you possess the speaking gifts of Sir Winston Churchill, then your good speech will take you about two weeks to write and rehearse.

Double or triple that for the rest of us.

3
How Do I Begin A Speech?

Begin with the end. The end is your main idea, the reason you wanted to speak in the first place. Reid Buckley[16] says they will remember nothing but your last utterance. Begin with it; end with it. You do not have to give everything away up front. Hint at the amazing revelation to be found when you conclude.

The audience will decide in the first ten seconds whether you are worth listening to. This makes it even more important to begin with the end, and make sure it is a grabber. You might even dispense with such niceties as how happy you are to be there, how generous they are to have you, or the obligatory *thank-you very much*. You have ten seconds. Do not waste it.

Begin your speech with the audience in mind. Put them in it. The more specific, the better. This is ordinary: *Air pollution is still a problem in our country. Each year, the number of pollutants we breathe is growing.*

This is better: *The people of Metropolis, all of us right now, are breathing poorer air today than one year ago.*

Best of all: *Please, would you all take a deep breath... Now, hold your breath...* Hold up a long list. *Here is the list of pollutants you now hold in your lungs.* Hold up a short list. *Here is that same list a year ago. Those who wish to may resume breathing.*

4
What's The Best Way To End A Speech?

End with the beginning. If your beginning was 1, 2, 3 make your ending 3, 2, 1. The end is a climax. You enthusiasm peaks. You are in the zone. You cannot pretend. You must be there. Your sentences are short; your pauses are long. This lets them know the end is coming.

---

[16] Mr. Buckley, brother of William F., is founder of the Buckley School of Public Speaking and author of *Strictly Speaking*.

A conclusion sings when your last utterance is about them, you, and your idea come together in perfect confluence.

5
How Should I Practice My Speech?

Practice your speech the same way you will deliver it. The closer you mimic actual performance conditions, the more valuable your practice time will be. Every show I staged included a dress rehearsal. At the very least, stand up and say it to one or two people a few times.

6
What If I Get Too Nervous?

The best way is to be so prepared that you are confident to the point of near arrogance: *My material kills, and I can do it my sleep.*

A few minutes before you speak, retire to a private place. A stall in the bathroom will do. Meditate, or pray, or breathe deeply (a nice clean rest room helps) for a minute. Better still, do all three.

Meditate on your message. Recall where you were when this idea came to you. Pray for the power to communicate your message with truth and humility. Breathe. Three deep breaths, each followed by a long slow exhalation, will calm your body down. If you take the time to do these three things, I guarantee you will be at your best.

7
What If The Staff Is Clearing Tables?

Servers are in a hurry to clear and leave. Chairmen are in a hurry to get the program underway. A simultaneous launch will nuke your attention grabbing opener.

The best time to deal with this is two weeks in advance. Mail your pre-speech checklist of requirements to the meeting chairperson. Arrive well in advance of your speaking time. Review your list again with the facility manager and event chairman. Behind-the-scenes people have the power to save you. At Gillette I traveled around the country setting up meeting rooms. I always befriended the men with serious tool belts and *"Jim"* sewn over their left pockets. A tip in advance may help.

Seek out the headwaiter at dinner functions. This is the person who will ride herd over the dish bangers. They will be firmly in your corner if you have made them your friend in advance. Before you ask for what you want, give them your time and respect. Honor their contribution to the event.

If your best efforts fail, then wait for quiet. If the noise is truly distracting, your audience will wait with you. However, do not be too much of a prima donna. Smile and speak up. Your flexibility and *the-show-must-go-on* attitude will endear you to the crowd. While you wait, do something physical. Move the furniture around. Go exchange business cards with the front row, or the nearest table. Christine Lavin would twirl her baton. Steve Martin would twirl his lasso. Marcel Marceau would get caught in a box. You could lead the audience in a relaxing *Tai-Chi* session. As the only person with a microphone, you own the room. Feel free to act as if you do. Then get on with it.

8
Should I Scout A Room?

What enables the wise sovereign and the good general to strike and conquer, and achieve beyond ordinary men, is foreknowledge.

Sun-Tsu, *The Art of War*

Research is that which you neglect at your peril. If you cannot check the room out personally well in advance, then show up early enough on speech day to have time to fix what needs fixing, or have an advance team do it for you.

Look for the light switch. It can be in another room behind a panel disguised to look like part of the wall. Sometimes only Jim knows where it is. He also knows where the air conditioning switch is, how to turn the heat up or down, and where the extra chairs are.

Look for tables and chairs that are where you want them, raised platforms that are high enough, and wide enough, and strong enough. You want a spring in your step, not in the platform.

Look for projectors that work, electrical outlets that are live, writing boards with markers and erasers to go with them. Keep a marker in your pocket, the wide black one, so you will have it when the ones you left there are not there. Look for flip charts that flip and that do not fall down. Have spares of everything. Not a spare bulb, a spare projector. Hire a technician to stand by if machines are a big part of the act. Make sure the technician knows that *stand by* means in the room, not in the building.

Look for microphones that do not howl when spoken into. Look for microphone holders that hold, stands that stand, height adjusters that do not go limp as you speak. Look for long cords. See that cords are taped down so you, and others, do not fall down.

After you have done everything you can think of, be prepared for that which you did not think of.

At the Intercontinental Hotel in New York, I had been on site for two days setting up a press conference. Gillette executives had come to introduce the new Sensor razor to Wall Street. Our new TV commercial, which had cost millions to develop and produce, was the centerpiece of the show. No expense was too outlandish to ensure that this meeting went off smoothly. I was authorized to spend whatever it took.

I rented a GE Lightvalve video projector and a mega sound system for $5,000 a day, and hired the owner to stand by at $500 per day. I asked him never to stray more than three feet from his technical marvel without letting me know. We rehearsed all day and all night. Perfection was in sight.

The next morning was showtime. White gloved attendants served delicate pastries on linen, and poured perfect coffee from tall silver services. Hands were shaken. Backs were thumped. Confident chuckles and commanding voices competed to command the room. Then the speeches and slides began.

Finally, the legendary John Symons introduced his new baby. *The* John Symons, who had jetted in from London the night before, and swept into the rehearsal room at 10PM with his entourage, shook my hand and said, "Ah, yes. Steve Rapson, I've heard so much."

Mr. Symons spoke lovingly about his new Gillette flagship brand, the Sensor razor. His reputation is that of an arrogant man, but he is winning them over with just the right mix of confidence and deference. He impresses the press.

"You are about to see the culmination of years of research. Millions of dollars of investment. A global commitment like no other... (yadah, yadah, yadah, as they say)... Roll that great new commercial, Steve."

The sound is terrific. It rattles the room. The assembled financial illuminati stare at a blank screen. Their heads swivel to the rear, to see if mine is rolling down the aisle. Still attached, with eyebrows painfully arched, my head swivels towards the $500 a day technician now dashing to the rear of his $5,000 a day machine that is eating my career.

After several moments, the great new commercial anti-climatically appears. In show business it does not matter why the show did not go on. It is only recalled that it not go on as planned.

At ten-thirty AM, four blocks away in mid-town Manhattan, a large building had collapsed. This caused an electrical spike to surge though trunk cables, down feeder lines into the electrical grids of nearby hotel meeting rooms, where expensive video devices hummed in warm readiness to fulfill their mission.

These video devices are so delicate and valuable that they are designed to detect nasty electrical spikes. Cleverly, they shut themselves off just in time to avoid burnout. In the unlikely event that this happens, a tiny red light on the back of the machine begins to blink. This blinking means, "press the reset button." If one's eyes are not glued to the back of the machine, one will not see the blinking and thus not press the reset button. The show will not go on as planned.

I do not remember the successful, uneventful shows I have staged. How well I remember this one.

9
Should I Hire A Speech Coach?

If you believe speaking is important to you and your business, you should work with a coach before the need arises. At Gillette, as in many organizations, speech coaches were sometimes brought in at the last minute to spruce up the speaker and the speech before a big presentation. This rarely works as hoped. It takes experience, preparation and practice to do what a coach advises. Usually there is little time to effect changes. On presentation day, the pressure is on, lessons are forgotten, and old habits return.

In the short run speech coaches try to minimize red flags and self-inflicted wounds to the feet. Often, a video session is used to help a client see how artificial mannerisms may keep them from being their best.

I set up the camera as soon as I walk in and secretly turn it on, saying, "I would like to video tape you at the lectern, delivering your speech. First, let's talk about your objectives."

We sit and chat about the weather, hobbies, and business. Then, I ask him to get up and deliver his speech to the camera. After the session, I hand the client the tape and say, "In order to document the complete you, the camera has been running since I arrived. Here is the only copy. No one will see it but you. Watch this tape by yourself. Make notes on what you like, and what you don't like about what you see."

Most people find who they are while sitting and chatting more palatable than the person they become on the podium. A lifetime of practice at being conversational makes you good at it. You have had less time being that way on a stage. A coach gives you the tools to behave naturally in an artificial environment.

10
How Should I Handle Interruptions?

A spontaneous question means someone is listening. It is natural for you to respond. A back and forth is desirable, and a rise from the crowd may be just what you want.

On the other hand, you may have a twenty-minute speech that you want to deliver *in toto*. You have a well honed act and you need your allotted time to do it. For example, a formal press conference where you are explaining to the press why you did (or did not do) that awful thing. Of course, they would rather hear you answer their pointed questions. You would rather say your piece first, then submit to a few questions.

If you are speaking to a large audience, more than fifty people, say, then there needs to be structure. The MC or Chairman will set the ground rules so you do not have to police the crowd. Others are there to do that for you. If the audience knows Q&A will follow, they will wait. If not, you are being heckled. See the first section for Question #98—*How to handle hecklers.*

11
How Should I Use Breaks?

Every book on public speaking advises brevity in public speech. Boring an audience is easy. Entertaining them is difficult. That is why experts advise keeping it short.

Simply imposing a limit on the duration of your remarks to twenty minutes will increase your odds of not boring them. Without writing a word, doing any research, or practice, you are ahead of those who go on too long.

All day seminars require more than breaks. Successful seminar people have three things in common:

First, they pack the goods. Expert speakers have the material to engage and interest their target audience. Audiences do not want re-hashed aphorisms, trite truisms, and long explanations of anything. Successful speakers and lecturers avoid these pitfalls by packing their words with substance, with personal revelation, fascinating anecdotes, and technical virtuosity. For example, the expert parachutist knows how to pack a chute so it will open every time. He knows how it feels to leap out of an aircraft, to see the earth rush up at 120 MPH, when to pull the cord, and how to land without breaking a leg. The audience wants to know these things, too. Personal revelations of secrets uncovered are the core of an interesting speech. People want truths they do not already know. As long as they are getting them, they will stay engaged.

Second, they break it up. An audience may be hungry enough to eat your whole horse. They will get sick if you feed it to them all at once. Most people will begin to squirm after forty minutes of any speaker. If they are not squirming they are enraptured, polite, or asleep.

Third, they involve the audience. Break the audience into smaller groups and get them involved. Have them solve a sample problem, encourage fire walking, hugging, and shouting. These techniques force camaraderie and break down isolation.

At the very least build a Q&A session into the program. If they will not ask questions then ask them yourself and then answer them. Speaker Jack Falvey tells his audience right up front that he wants to make sure they get what they came for. He asks, "What do you want to make sure I cover before we are finished?" He gets them involved and thinking early on. This is necessary because they are, in the end, responsible for their own learning.

Mortimer Adler observed that, of all the professions, doctors, farmers, and teachers share a unique quality: they ply their skills on patients, soil, and students; however, they do not control the outcome. It is the responsibility of the body to heal, the seed to grow, and student to learn. A breakout session is where the audience, the students, begin to do their part.

12
What If I Get A Signal To Stop?

Did you go over the agreed upon time? Skip to the end and wrap it up. It is good form to finish in the allotted time, or even a few minutes earlier. It is necessary if others are on the program. Opening acts will not open again for anyone whose audience they burned out by going on too long.

I attended a Toastmaster's meeting recently where a young woman presented her five to seven minute *persuasive* speech. A timekeeper sat at the back of the room and held up helpful little signs. First was *TWO MINUTES...* then *ONE MINUTE...* then *TIME'S UP.* The speaker continued. The final sign said **PLEASE STOP!** She continued for another three minutes while staring at **PLEASE STOP!** The compulsion to finish saying what we think needs saying destroys our sense of time. I can assure you it crawls for the captive listener.

In a final appeal for brevity, Reid Buckley advises, "The audience will forget your thesis by the time you have answered the last question." Therefore, always have an anecdote that sums up your main idea. Then you may skip to it at any time.

13
When Should I Hand Out My Materials?

Hand out materials after your speech. You want them looking at you, not flipping through your handouts. If your talk is technical, with charts and graphs, then use a slide or overhead projector. Turn it on, show the graphic, turn it off. Put blank slides between your charts, if you do not want to turn the projector on and off. When a graphic is on the screen, their attention is diverted from you. By managing your visuals you keep the audience looking where you want them to.

If you are not teaching science, there is little justification for myriad graphs, formulae and pictures. There is no justification for graphics that contain the words you are saying. It is true that we retain more of what we see, but not what we are compelled to read.

Most speakers use visual aids to lessen the load on them. They are busy, so they prepare less. The audience is forced to sit in a dark room watching pretty slides blink on and off while the speaker hides behind the lectern providing a dull audio track.

14
Can I Change The Topic?

Speakers must have a passion for their subject, and have written and practiced for several days—if not months and years. If the event needs a speaker on A, and you have not thought much about A, then suggest B (your baby) or decline. Avoid surprises, unless you are bombing.

15
May I Ask For Addresses To Follow-Up?

If you speak or entertain for a living, your mailing list is the engine that propels your career. Make it easy for people to give you their contact information. Have a jar for business cards, and a sign up sheet that is passed among the audience. Create an inducement for your audience to stay in touch with you. Have free books and tapes, a newsletter of your own, a website with a guest book. Get there early and meet everybody in advance. Exchange business cards with them. The hardest work pays the highest dividend.

Motivational sales trainer, G. Worthington Hipple began his presentation to Gillette sales reps with a personal greeting. He knew their name, sales territory and a bit of personal background about each and every one of them.

"Good morning, Bill. Bill Smith is it?" He said, shaking hands. "I'm George Hipple. Pleased to meet you, and thanks for coming. How big is that Indianapolis territory? You get in some fly fishing out there?"

He makes this part of his act. Hipple requests a brief bio on each sales rep in advance of the meeting, which he memorizes the night before. With the sales reps sitting in alphabetical order, he goes around the room. This may seem like a gimmick; but, with pre-planning, it is a powerful way to connect with a smaller audience. Later Hipple asks them why they think he did it.

"It was not easy," he said, "I spent all evening learning about each of you. I did it because this presentation was important to me. I wanted you to like me, and remember what I will tell you this morning. By showing you my commitment, I gain your trust and favorable attention."

He was making a selling point that applied equally well to speech making. As a final bonus for his work, he added a dozen pre-sold names to his mailing list.

16
What If I Am Completely Bombing?

If you are sure you are not going over, this is useful knowledge. Most ineffective speakers are clueless that they are boring. They tough it out, even when they have lost the crowd, grinding forward in lockstep towards certain failure. If you know death is waiting in the wings, then take a chance and do something else. Search for serendipity; toss the script and go with your gut. I mean this figuratively, but wouldn't it be great to have a pile of loose papers to toss in the air?

Although winging it is fraught with risk, you might as well try if nothing else is working. Reach within yourself and summon the resources that a lifetime of work and study have given you. Do not die easily. Take deep breath and think on your feet. Be humble, not humiliated. Although it feels like it is all about you; it is not. The audience owns some of what is happening.[17]

---

[17] 50% of your success or failure belongs to the audience. You cannot know their individual prejudices, and it is not possible to be different each night to fit

Stop, look around, and ask a provocative question. Employ some bits of business while you think. Take off your coat. Loosen your tie. Remove your earrings. Let your hair down. Stretch. Encourage the audience to do the same. Walk close to the people. Put your hands on your hips and stare at them as if you can read their minds. Whatever you were doing, do the opposite. You are bombing. What could hurt?

Comedians use a saver when a joke bombs. A saver is what you say immediately after a remark that elicits silence instead of the laugh it was intended to get. Here is one from Don White. He speaks sotto voce into the mike while miming a notepad:

"When in (*name of town*) avoid existentialist references."

Mary Gauthier says:

"Oh, boy! You're making my dreams come true tonight!"

I play solo guitar. If I make several mistakes in a row I say, while playing:

"Some of these notes are right!" It always gets a laugh and keeps everybody relaxed, me included.

Not doing comedy? Are you bombing while trying to retain your budget for the next fiscal year? Outlining your marketing plan for the new VP? Appealing to the zoning board to not take your private road? Skip to your main point, and, in sixty seconds, say, *Here is what I want. Here is what's in it for you. Thank you very much.* Be done and get out of there.

17
What If A Podium Is Not Available?

A podium is the raised platform you stand upon, the better to be seen by the crowd. A lectern is a high desk with a slanted top, the better to hide behind. If you are not reading your speech, there is no need for a lectern. Unlike children, speakers should be heard *and* seen.

---

what you think they want. A friend of mine is a nationally known speaker. He is great in ability and in size: not tall, he weighs over 350 pounds. A woman told him after a speech, "I would never pay attention to a person who looks like you." This hurt, and he told me so. It is tough out there, even for those who know it and succeed anyway.

The best use of a lectern is the dramatic effect one gets by walking out from behind it. It is worth asking for one just so you may do that.

18
What If People Walk Out?

They are leaving for reasons of their own; ignore them. It may have nothing to do with you or your speech. If you say good-bye to early exitors, or make light of them in some way, it always comes off as small and beneath you. When you hold the microphone, you have a certain power over the room. Abusing that power makes you look bad. Even if you are the boss and the troops are heading for the links and the bar early, ignore them for now. Take names for later. However, if you are the third comedian on the bill at Harry's Ha-Ha Hut, destroy them.

I was on the receiving end of abuse from the podium when Allen Rosenshine, CEO of BBDO Worldwide, spoke to a hundred Gillette marketers. When he said, "Roll that commercial, Steve," the projector failed. As I scrambled at the back of the room, Rosenshine made little quips about inept media people. Although a polished speaker, he was nervous and annoyed; his joking to stay calm at my expense was in poor form. I could see this, even through my own distress. As did John Darman, who rose and said, "Why don't we all take a little break," saving me from further barbs.

I now publicly thank the classy and nimble Mr. Darman, and finally forgive Mr. Rosenshine.

19
Should I Speak Before or After Dinner?

I do not know which is worse: to speak to a group so hungry they can not attend to your speech, or to a group so stuffed and comatose they cannot attend to your speech.

If it is your show, you have all the say. If you are mildly famous you have some say. Usually the program committee has the say. After dinner speakers have survived for a few centuries. So will you.

20
Is It OK To Read A Speech?

If your speech is destined to become public or corporate policy, if it has the force of law, if you can be held to account for what you say, if what you will say outweighs how you say it, then read it.

21
Is It Possible To Be Too Funny?

No, but it is possible to try too hard to be funny.

If the humor is about you and your foibles, if it is true, if it is germane to your message, then rolling in the aisles is a good place for your audience to be.

If you are using canned jokes shoehorned into your presentation as comic relief, then you may not be too funny at all. I recommend Judy Carter's book, *How To Be a Stand-Up Comedian*. This is not to be a comedian, but to understand the craft that underlies effective use of humor.

I have seen hundreds of beginning speakers and performers fail to be amusing. They fail most completely when they try to be amusing. They fail because they do not trust the audience to get it, and they spoon feed it to them. Through body language, facial expression, tone of voice, and pace, the jokester broadcasts that a laugh is coming. This is called asking for the laugh. Biblical promises notwithstanding, if you ask, you will not receive.

When poor performance is paired with poor material, which is why the lame jokes are in there, the hapless speaker gets the dreaded sympathy laugh. Lower than the polite laugh: *I can see how others might find that funny, ha... ha... ha... the sympathy laugh means, I am embarrassed for you; I'll try to laugh... eh, eh, heh, eehh.*

22
When Should I Use Visual Aids?

Great speakers connect with their audience, and visual aids hinder that connection. The people must be looking at you and you at them. If you are both looking at a screen, no connection will occur. Although slides and overheads are supposed to simplify and clarify complex information, I think it is better to first work on your words to make your ideas clear and simple.

During the Clinton impeachment trial, house prosecutors used huge charts to make their case. In contrast, Dale Bumpers opened the President's defense with a 53-minute speech and no visuals. No one remembers much of the House prosecutors' opening remarks. Bumper's speech, however, was praised in the national press for its brilliant defense of Clinton, whose behavior was, most said, indefensible. In addition to its flawless technical construction, Bumper's speech was filled with sympathy and empathy for a President and his family who were receiving very little of either from that same press.

Charts, slides, and pretty pictures should not be what you are about when you stand up to connect with the people. Visuals can support the point. They should not be the point. If your objective is to move the audience so that they remember what you say, and do what you wish them to do, then stand up and talk to them directly. The technical side has its place before and after, but not during your speech.

In the courtroom, jurors listen to testimony and view physical evidence, but not simultaneously. Lawyers stop talking while physical evidence is shown to the jury. When a lawyer wants to make a powerful point with a visual, he usually brandishes it in his hand while speaking emotionally about the facts of the case. Defense council Johnny Cochran took abuse for wearing O.J. Simpson's wool cap during his summation. What I saw was a master presenter making his point unforgettable to the jury, and unforgettable to millions who saw him on TV.

23
How Do I Quiet An Audience?

Stand up straight. Do not look down. Look out on the crowd with a pleasant expectant expression on your face, as if you are waiting for order and quiet—and fully expect it—before you begin. Your gaze can linger on those who have yet to notice you. Soon they will be quiet; say nothing until they are.

24
Should I Write My Own Introduction?

Your bio is the source document for introductions. It is the duty of the introducer to condense it into a brief introduction. They should include some detail about the group you are addressing, to help them answer the question, *Why should I listen to you?* I have seen introductions fail because the introducer has done no preparation. They squint and hesitate over hastily scribbled notes. Therefore, it is a good idea to have a concise, generic introduction ready to hand to them at the last minute, if needed.

25
How Important Is Eye Contact?

Love at first sight depends upon the looking. The demure among us glance away fleetingly when we contact a stranger's eyes. When you speak, you cannot look away.

In high school I always won the staring contests because I learned to look right into another's eyes by concentrating on the bridge of their nose, between their eyes. That is how to do it up close; it avoids shifty eyes. Further away, focus on one face in a group. People nearby will feel as if you are looking directly at them, too.

Eye connection is the first step to mind connection which leads to heart and soul connection. It takes time and commitment to hold your gaze on another, to really look at them. Do not let your eyes drift aimlessly, without focussing on any one face. No one will feel as if you looked at them, and thus no connection.

Eye contact is hard to do for the same reason we are judicious about it in everyday life. It is risky. We look at others to evaluate their character as, simultaneously, they do the same to us. This is an uncomfortable feeling.

Eyes are the windows to the soul.[18] When we look into an audience member's eyes we feel most exposed and vulnerable, and so may they. We must do it to make a personal connection. You may not win them all, but you will win enough of them.

26
How Can I Improve My Voice?

The easiest way to improve your voice is to read aloud every day. Try to read slowly, with long pauses. Poetry is ideal material for this, as are great speeches from history. Your own upcoming speech, if read aloud many times, will take on a relaxed sonority that your normal speaking may lack. Also, read without emphasis, and do not try to sell the words. Let them speak for themselves and you will sound conversational. Because, as you become familiar with the speech, your natural speaking rhythm will emerge out without any special effort.

If you have physical limitations that prevent you from speaking clearly, a vocal therapist will help. If you take singing lessons, and do the exercise you are given, your speaking voice will improve as a side benefit. See voice therapist Mark Baxter, at www.voicelesson.com.

---

[18] "These lovely lamps, these windows of my soul." Du Bartas. 1544-1590. (From his "Divine Weekes and Workes," translated by J. Sylvester.)

27
Should I Tailor My Remarks To Local Issues?

Beyond a nodding appreciation of the land, and a respect for its people, I would avoid injecting local color or issues into your talk. Your audience knows considerably more about their issues than you do. If you skim the local paper a few days before you speak, your references may appear shallow, or infer a depth of understanding you lack. Either way, you risk putting them off, which is the opposite of your goal of connecting with them.

28
How Is A Good Speech Organized?

The author Elmore Leonard said, *"When you write, try to leave out all the parts readers skip."* Pity the listener who cannot skip.

If you include too much, no organizing system will help. Many speakers make the mistake of inundating their audience with, "THAT WHICH MUST BE SAID." They are afraid that if something is left out, their meaning might be lost or misconstrued. I suggest to clients, "Write down ten things you wish them to know. Pretend they can remember only three. Which three will you choose?"

"I can't do that," they say, "this is a complex subject."

"If you include too much, as in, *...And another crucial element...* it is likely they will remember nothing. Three is the limit and one of those must predominate."

Decide what is to be communicated, and then organize it. I suggest beginning with the end, and ending with the beginning. This is similar to the organizing cliché is: *First, tell 'em what you are going to tell 'em. Next, tell 'em. Finally, tell 'em what you told 'em.* Another one is: *Get an attention grabbing introduction, and a stirring climax. Put them as close together as possible.*

How your speech is organized is less important than the fact that it is, in some way, organized. For example, if you stack concrete blocks in random piles, or even one great pile, you may wonder how many blocks are there. With no pattern to the stack, you must count each one.

Similarly, your speech is a collection of ideas that, if organized in some pattern, are easier to recall as parts of a coherent whole. The steps to your conclusion ascend logically towards your one big idea.

Speech organizing patterns are best if they are simple. In fact, the more complex your topic, the simpler your organizing theme should be:

Corporate/personal growth.
1. What was it like?
2. What happened?
3. What is it like now?

The great new/old thing.
1. What's good about it?
2. What's bad about it?
3. What about it?

Issue of the day.
1. What does it mean to you?
2. What does it mean to them?
3. What does it all mean?

Chronological
1. Last week, this.
2. This week, that.
3. Next week, the other thing.

The fix we (they, you) are in.
1. How did we (they, you) get in it?
2. How do we (they, you) get out?
3. How do we (they, you) stay out?

Geographical ordering
1. North. Here
2. South. There.
3. East & West. Everywhere.

The audience expects you to take care of them, to do all the heavy lifting. They are lazy listeners. You make it easy for them with a clear pattern to your ideas.

29
Should The Audience Tape Me?

The Grateful Dead encouraged it. If you are as relaxed about your performance as they were, go ahead.

If people make a recording, ask those who do to send you a good copy. You can trade with them for one you recorded elsewhere. Your collection and their's will benefit.

30
What is The Difference Between Speaking To An Audience Of 10 Or A 1,000?

The main difference is that we think there is a difference. A huge crowd may cause us to oversell, or trigger stage fright. Again, it is only because of thinking too much. Managing our normal feelings just before we go on is an important part of becoming an effective speaker.

For me, small audiences are tougher then large ones. The intimacy of a small group makes me feel like covering up. I lose my concentration because their individuality tends to make me think about each one of them. Also, a group of ten may be more inclined to interrupt. A large crowd is more anonymous, I think of them less; so, paradoxically, I feel more at ease.

When you address a thousand people from a high stage, your instinct is to be more expansive, to project your voice too much. It takes discipline to maintain a conversational tone, but still project. In addition, it is harder to make meaningful eye contact.

Other than that, there is little difference.

31
Should I Memorize My Speech?

With the exception of Bill Clinton or Ronald Reagan reading from a teleprompter, I have yet to see a speaker read a speech and connect with an audience. As difficult as it is to get *off the page*, it is the best way to be effective.

In 1980 Ted Turner came to Boston to pitch his SuperStation idea to Gillette senior management. He arrived at the boardroom an hour before show time and handed me his 3/4" videocassette. As he inspected the room, I previewed the tape in the booth.

"Excuse me, Mr. Turner," I called, "does this tape have an audio track?"

He appeared in the doorway, "Of course it has audio."

"If it does, I can't find it," I said.

"I played that tape in New York yesterday, and there was audio then. What did you do?

"This machine is a player only. It can't erase anything."

"You must have done something. Fix it," he said.

He is in my face, four inches shorter, and muscling into my space.

I said, "The Chairman and President of Gillette are going to walk through that door in a few minutes. You are abusing the only one in this building who can help you." I am still proud of that line.

Ted smiled and held up both his hands like I had a gun on him.

"You're right. I'm sorry," he said, "What can you do. How can I help?"

I put a known good tape in the machine while Ted fiddled with the monitor in the boardroom. It had audio.

"Looks like your tape is bad. I can't give you audio that's not there," I said.

"Somebody's in trouble," he said, adding, "You want a job in Atlanta?"

"No thanks, I'm happy here."

"OK," he said, "Here's what we're going to do."

Turner shook hands with Gillette executives as they filed in. His celebrity got him this face time, but he had to give a good pitch to get the order. Although videotape was a key part of his presentation (which I generally do not recommend) I think he gave a better speech because of the lost audio. After some genial opening remarks where he explained the technical problem, he said, "Steve, roll the tape."

"Well, there I am sitting behind my big desk. Makes me look even shorter. What I'm saying here is…"

Turner had his pitch down, and narrated the tape flawlessly. He was relaxed and jocular about it, and warmed the room up more than anyone who graced Gillette's boardroom before.

32
Do I Dress Up For A Speech?

Many corporations have gone to casual dress for day-to-day work at the office. Business attire is still required when traveling. A high quality business suit for men or women is always appropriate. Anything less might not be. Do not take a chance on not making a good first impression, which begins when they first see you. Even if they tell you dress is casual, still wear your best suit. You can always take off your coat and roll up your sleeves.

33
How Do I To Deliver A Speech To A Hostile Audience?

In writing. Failing that, do everything recommended here.

34
What Should I Do In A TV Interview?

Lower your volume a little. On stage you project to a few dozen or a few thousand people. On television you are speaking to one or two people on the other side of the lens. Therefore, you are at your best when you speak naturally, as if they were sitting across from you.

You cannot make a mistake as long as you stick to the un-varnished, un-spun truth about you. A skilled interviewer can sneak up on you from any direction, if that is their mission. There is only one way to survive intact and on top, and that is to tell the truth, laced with humor directed at yourself. It is a bulletproof vest.

You may not be able to tell the whole truth, but be prepared with what truth you will tell, and what you will not. I recommend you read Roger Ailes' book, *You Are The Message*. His advice on surviving an interview is excellent. In a nutshell, he says to have a three-tiered answer for each issue. Reporters probe by asking the same question in different forms. Each of your brief answers should give a bit more information. If you are pressed further, after your three answers, you return to the first answer, "…as I said before…" and go through them all again. It is an excellent way to stay "on message."

Be prepared for the obvious: "Don't they eat a lot of hay?" Every elephant salesman is sure to get this question. The successful ones are prepared to answer it.

Former Vice-President Dan Quayle demonstrated to a national audience the price of poor preparation. On CBS's *48 Hours,* he was asked if he thought his reputation as a buffoon—inaccurate, but well-earned—would haunt him throughout his political career? His face darkened, "No," was all he said

Mr. Quayle had an opportunity to lighten up on this issue and start turning his image around. He blew it. How could this happen? Surely this appearance on *48 Hours* had been on his schedule for weeks. Had not his staff been analyzing this issue of *Dan The Clown*? Did they not have a plan for defusing it? What were they thinking?

If Dan Quayle had been my client, I would have suggested the following when that inevitable question was posed:

Smile, laugh even, and say, "Well, when people remember the silly gaffs, I hope they'll also remember the serious issues I care about, like... *(list issues)*... I'll keep reminding them... carefully."

Alternatively, after the smile, "Well, the Dan Quayle Story is still being written. The first chapters feature a lot of laughs. In the next ones I hope to bring serious attention to... *(list issues.)"*

Or, again, after the smile, "I know what you mean. We all have feet of clay. Sometimes it looks like I have a head of clay to match. But I don't mind if I can continue to put forth issues important to all Americans, like...*(list issues.)"*

The truth shot up with a laugh is an unbeatable combination. Humor does not mean you are not serious about your subject. It means you do not take yourself so seriously that you cannot even laugh at your own foibles.

When you prepare for an interview, identify what you are most afraid of answering, and then practice the answer to it. If you cannot talk about certain issues, then say so. However, be prepared with the three things you *can* say. If there is nothing you can say, how did you get in this awkward position—a camera in your face—in the first place?

Never argue or lose your cool; and never say to a reporter, "Shut-up and listen to me for a minute," as did the Chairman of the Democratic Party at the 2000 convention. The media will lead with your outburst every time. Alternatively, knowing this, you may *want* to be controversial, secure in the knowledge that your most outrageous remarks will air.

35
How Do I Make A Toast?

It gives me great pleasure. — G. B. Shaw

George Bernard Shaw offered this toast during a fashionable English dinner party. Back then, it was customary for the host to appoint the toaster, as well as supply the subject. Since sex was an unmentionable in polite society at the turn of the century, this was an amusing attempt to tongue-tie Shaw and quash his legendary wit. The ruse failed, and his clever toast lives on a hundred years later.

Today, toasting is less formal, and the worse for it. As an MC and bandleader, I have witnessed thousands of toasts. Most toasters were self-conscious and ill at ease. Best men at weddings, business people, professors, and woozy after-dinner hosts have all missed their opportunity to be their best, to say and do the right thing, and to honor themselves and their guests.

A toast is a mini speech, and the same rules apply as for a big speech. If you find it painful to stand in front of people all looking at you—and you cannot get out of doing the toast—then do the following:

Write and memorize a two-line toast, For example:

"To Bill and Mindy... health and happiness. Cheers."

Now you must practice it exactly as you will do it. Stand up, stand tall, and stand still. Practice picking up the glass while holding the microphone. Look at the person being toasted, and at the assembled guests. Take three deep breaths before you speak. Speak with a firm clear voice.

Always stand before offering a toast, unless it is a small informal group. Standing will get the attention of the group and quiet them down. Don't tap on your glass. It is considered slightly gauche in some circles. Hold your glass up and wait for quiet. You might say, "A toast..." to encourage attention.

Never refuse to participate in a toast. It is more polite, and perfectly acceptable, to participate with a non-alcoholic beverage, or even an empty glass. A traditional woman once refused to toast to my glass of water, "I never toast to water," she said. It is an old custom and one best not adhered to so publicly.

If you honor your duty as a toast giver, you not only honor yourself and the toastee, you show respect for everyone who hears your words.

36
Should I List With A Speaker's Bureau?

If they will have you, it couldn't hurt. Do not pay to be listed, this means they are in the business of listing you for a fee, not placing you with paying clients. Most speakers get work through their own personal network of business and social contacts. Top speakers usually have an agent, or staff, who handles appearance requests.

The usual route for speakers are freebies at the local Chamber of Commerce, Rotary, high school and college programs, or anywhere they will have you. As you improve, your references and callbacks will get better and better. Soon you will have to start charging to keep the number of engagements down.

37
Where Can I Meet Other Speakers

Here are several resources available on the Internet. They will lead you to people and places that will you to help work on your act.

www.nsaspeaker.org —The National Speakers Association is an organization of people who speak for a living. Their newsletter is SpeakerNet News: The Weekly Resource for the Professional Speaking Community. It goes out each Friday to 2000 professional speakers, consultants, trainers, and authors.

www.nespeakers.com — The New England Division of NSA.

www.speaking.com/articlesspeakers—You will find information on successful speakers, and articles about how to do it yourself.

www.toastmasters.org is a non-profit corporation headquartered in Rancho Santa Margarita, California. Local club meetings help people improve their public speaking skills. If you would like to attend a meeting, telephone Toastmasters International World Headquarters at (714) 858-8255 and ask for the location of a club near you. Write them at Toastmasters International, P.O. Box 9052, Mission Viejo CA 92690.

38
What's The Difference Between A Good And Bad Lecturer?

Bad lecturers use long sentences.

Your sentences will be short and your words simple. You will avoid the passive and conditional voice: verbs with an *ing* at the end and phrases like, *there is, could be drawn,* or *it is to be hoped.* Shun *-tion* words.

Bad lecturers are long on ideas and short on examples.

You will leap from example to story in a single bound. You will tell stories and give examples till the cows come home.

Bad lecturers drone on because there is so much to say and so little time.

You, the good lecturer, will look for every opportunity to let silence spread over the room. You will ask questions of the audience. You will wait a long time for an answer. You will command the silence.

Bad lecturers, on the rare occasion they attempt humor, advertise that a laugh is coming.

Their body language and facial expressions scream, "Here comes that funny line I have been working so hard to deliver riiii-ght... HERE!" Everybody sees it coming. Nobody is surprised; few are amused.

You will never do that. You will be a sneaky bastard. You will frown in advance of the laugh. You will lower your voice on the punch line. When the audience laughs you will stop speaking, surprised that something funny has been said. If they do not laugh, your stoic demeanor will save you from being the only person in the room with a grin on his face.

Bad lecturers surprise in one way: The end, differing in no way from the rest of the speech, catches the audience blinking in surprise.

This is not you. They don't call it the climax for nothing. You are going to let them know it is coming. You are going to increase your volume and emotional commitment. You are going to go out fast and strong. You will have something saved for the end that will make them glad they stayed to hear it.

Bad lecturers do not listen.

You listen so that you will be in tune your audience and simpatico with how they are feeling. You will check in on them with a question, the answer to which you will wait.

Bad lecturers run overtime.

You will be done before they expect it. If you are asked to give a thirty-minute speech, you will prepare a twenty-minute speech. Or a fifteen minute speech. Voltaire said, "Woe to the author determined to teach. The secret of being a bore is to tell everything." You are a good lecturer when you save something for the Q&A or the after-speech cocktail party.

Your reward for being an uncommonly good lecturer is threefold.

First, your audience will be attentive throughout, and happily surprised at the end.

Second, there is time for Q&A. If you know your subject, and the audience has an interest, Q&A is always better than a lecture. Q&A is your encore.

Third, because of your brevity and focus they may remember what you said and tell others. Word of mouth is the way important messages have been carried for all time. There is the tale of a murder in London at midnight. Two witnesses happen upon the scene. Fifteen minutes later they each tell two others who similarly tell two others, and so on. If this continues, everyone on earth will know of it by morning.

SUMMING UP

Summing Up

Knowing the rules of an art is not the same as having the habit. When we speak of a man as skilled in any way, we do not mean that he knows the rules of making or doing something, but that he possesses the habit of making or doing it. The art as something that can be taught consists of rules to be followed into operation. The art as something learned and possessed consists of the habit that results from operating according to the rules.

Mortimer Adler & Charles Van Doren
From *How to Read a Book*

"Does it work?" You might reasonably ask. Deep breathing in restroom stalls, cultivating humility, and looking at people as if you know them. Or pretending that all is in control, when it feels out of control. Endless practice, and adherence to what you have practiced.

I had the chance to beta-test these ideas on a trip to North West Africa. Fear of failure drove me to it, and here is my report.

I traveled to Morocco with my friend Bill FitzPatrick. He was to give a graduation speech at the High-Tech School in Rabat, and bestow degrees at the ceremony; I was along for the ride. The day before, we had lunch the with the president of the school: the youthful, multi-lingual Zouhare, "Say *zoo* and *hair*," he instructed. We were crowded into a charming Moroccan bistro where French, Arabic, and English mingled around the table. I resorted to my usual smiling and nodding. I was, however, proud of my vestigial French when I asked for, and was directed to, the upstairs bathroom. During dessert Zouhare asked if I would play guitar after the graduation. As we left the restaurant, Bill said, "Rapson, do you know what you have agreed to?"

"A few songs after dinner at Zouhare's house."

"Not the house. The graduation ceremony."

I must have nodded when I should have smiled. I imagined my own graduation from Simmons College concluding with, "Now here is Etienne from Morocco to play guitar for you." Moroccan graduations are just like the American version, and I was nervous about how appropriate an impromptu concert would be.

The main hall of the Rabat Hilton was set up for five-hundred people. There was a raised dais with seating for professors and dignitaries across the front of the room. I sat in the hall as it filled with students and relatives. Older women were either completely robed and veiled, with neither hair nor skin showing, or wore only scarves. However, the younger men and women looked as if they had stepped out of *Cosmopolitan* or *GQ*. I gave up my seat so several people could sit together, and went out into the foyer, now buzzing with the overflow crowd. Except for the French and Arabic conversation, and older people in robes, it could have been Anywhere, USA.

The ceremony got under way with speeches and applause for the graduates. My impending performance seemed even more inappropriate, and I would have reverted to an impromptu speech, if only my French were better. I mingled with the crowd, pretending to be one of them. The day before, Bill and I had taken the train to Marrakech and toured the old market. A shopkeeper had dressed me in robes and *gutra* (the traditional Arab headdress) and said something in Arabic to his assistant, who laughed. "What?" I said.

"I told him that you looked like a Saudi," he said.

"Is that good?"

He answered with a hand waggle.

Although I did not buy the robes, I was confident that I blended in with the graduation guests: a Saudi uncle in Western clothes.

As the time neared, I unpacked my guitar and went into the men's room. Looking in the mirror, I wondered what advice would I offer a fellow performer in this situation?

Relax and get out of yourself. I did some deep breathing, meditated for a few minutes, and felt much better.

Connect with the people. Exiting the bathroom, I stopped trying to blend in. I made eye contact and smiled at whoever looked at me; many did, as I stood there conspicuously wearing a guitar. The background drone from inside the hall became coherent for an instant, *"...Steve Rapson..."* This was my cue, which caught me by surprise.

The logistics are not good; the aisles are packed, and I cannot get through. *"Excusez-moi... Pardonez-moi... Hello... Merci..."* I hugged my guitar close and slowly squeezed through the people in the aisle. Bill told me later he thought I had chickened out, and was hiding in my room. Halfway down the aisle, I broke though the press of the crowd. Fighting the impulse to hurry I ambled like a Saudi prince, greeting people seated to my right and left. Everyone returned my smile. The dais was crammed with tables and black-robed professors, and there was no place for me to stand. This was my punishment for not checking the room out in advance. However, there was a lectern on the floor to the right. I made that my goal.

Get on with it. Arriving up front, Bill and Zouhare stood to make room for me up on the dais, but I knew this would take too long. The lectern had a mike; I leaned into it and said in fractured French, *"Bonjour, Madames et Messieurs. Congratulationnes a la graduates..."*

The room exploded with laughter. I had made them laugh, though I was not sure how. Afterwards, a young man told me that there is no such word as *congratulations* in French. I had tried to make it sound French-like and they thought I was a mimicking an inept Englishman.

Make it for them. "Maintenant, je jouerai le High-Tech Graduate Blues." (Now, I will play...). At the word *blues,* they cheered. Blues is the universal music, and music is the universal language. I took a chance and improvised an introduction on an Arabic scale. I had practiced this in my room earlier. They loved it; and then I launched into a honky-tonk blues riff in A. All five-hundred people clapped along. I had thought about improvising lyrics, but finally did chicken out.

Be brief; be done. It was a race to finish before they stopped clapping. I played two choruses and ended just in time. *"Merci beaucoup, et bonsoir."* I got a standing ovation, and they crowded around for autographs and pictures. I felt like a star; and, as far as I can tell, there is no difference between being a star and just feeling like one.

I conclude that it works.

Successful people form the habit of doing that which no one likes to do. No one likes skim milk the first time. No one likes to exercise regularly. No one likes to take risks, or to be to be rejected. No one likes to get up early and work fourteen-hour days. No one likes to remember names, write thank-you notes, or be criticized. Successful people habitually do these things. Fortunately, although acquiring a good habit may be difficult, it is easy and automatic once we have it.

I joined the YMCA in Boston to swim after work, and found the pool too crowded. I tried 6:00AM. Voila! A lane to myself for a full hour. I did not like rising at 4:30AM; however, I truly enjoyed a leisurely swim with a big pool all to myself.

These suggestions for stage and podium success are common sense. We may know them, but acquiring the habit of doing them is the challenge. Only five percent of us, when presented with a course of action that could lead to a positive outcome, will take that action. However, when you *take* the road less traveled and *do* what nobody wants to do, you will find the road wide open. There are no crowds or lines, and no need to take number.

The competition is overwhelming only at the bottom where everybody starts. If you stick with it, you will leave most of the competition behind and find plenty of room above the fray. Sticking with it is hard, improving is hard, and changing is hardest of all.

Albert Einstein said the definition of insanity is continuing to do the same thing while expecting a different result. I harp on this because I have seen many performers and speakers who seem unable to modify what they do on stage. And the irony is that most need to do less, rather than more, or differently. My advice to many performers is to say less, move less, and express with the face less. Let the material speak for itself, and do not worry about how you are doing.

Recently, on PBS's, *Talk of the Nation,* Reid Buckley said, "Effective speakers are those able to suppress their ego, to engender a humility of spirit." He believes a lack of ego, and subjugation to your ideas is the surest way to connect. As you must know by now, this mirrors my point of view precisely. Along with a humility of spirit, I recommend persistence and focus. It is amazing what we can accomplish with a little effort in the same direction every day. Sometimes we find even a little effort, everyday, too much. We search for easier ways, and buy books that promise to reveal the secrets. However, I regret to say there are no secrets, except, of course, for the few revealed here.

It is my hope and wish that you found this book helpful, and that your success might be hastened because of it.

Acknowledgements

"You ought to write a book about performing," said Bill FitzPatrick, my friend, mentor, and client, after a consulting session.
"There are plenty of books already," I said.
"Not one by you."
Bill continued to nag me. I continued to ignore him. Then he dropped a pile of papers in front me, "Your book should be 101 Questions & Answers On Performing. Here are the questions. I've done most of the work for you. All you have to do is write the answers." His action spurred me to begin. Thank you, Bill. And thank you:

My friend and mentor, Jack Falvey, who edited early versions with skill, enthusiasm, and compassion.

My friends— Karen FitzPatrick, Ann Eder-Mulhane, Larry Richards, Steve Sullivan, Eliza Wyatt, Paul Chi, John Shockey, Steve Friedman, Mercedes Seldon, Ken Batts, Ron Harding, Granville Toogood, Jane Fallon, Peter Brewer, Paul Donehue, Bill Thibodeau, Howard Wight, and Kyle Shiver—all who read work-in-progress and gave wise council.

Don White, who made me laugh and cry when I first saw him perform at the Colonial Inn in Concord, Massachusetts. *Who is this guy?* He showed me the potential and power of the art.

Mary Gauthier and Kevin So, who went to countless open mikes with me. We learned together, and their success I enjoy vicariously.

Bill Hill, who played guitar in his dorm room at the University of Maine in 1966. I walked in and asked him to show me how he did it. He has been showing me ever since.

My friends Bob Fields and Lisa McCarthy, whose agency, Commonwealth Creative Associates, and designer Tracey Deshayes, create beautiful book and CD covers. Thank you, Bob, for your support. Thank you, Lisa, for the gift.

Ellen Schmidt, who gave me my first gig as a soloperformer.

Christine Lavin, who loved my book and told me so.

My daughters, Jill and Alicia. Whenever I think I must do something great in this life, I look at them and know I already have.

My wife, Rosemary, who is such a deep well of love, support and acceptance that, after thirty years, I have come to believe it is infinite.

Contributors

Ann Eder-Mulhane is the host of Java Jo's Open Mike where she provides a friendly atmosphere for new acts to work on their craft.

Steven Friedman owns Melville Park Studio in Boston. He holds a Ph.D. in physics, and combines his expertise in the science of sound with his love of acoustic music. He has produced recordings for artists such as Vox 1, Martin Sexton, Kerri Powers, and Vance Gilbert. www.melvillepark.com.

Mary Gauthier is a singer/songwriter based in Boston. Her performances, songwriting, and recordings have received universal acclaim from the country's toughest critics. www.marygauthier.com.

Ron Harding is the author of two books on creativity and communication. He is a professor at Boston University and president of Harding & Company. rhard@idt.net.

Don White is a singer/songwriter from Lynn, Massachusetts. He inspires his audience; and he inspired me as I wrote this book. www.donwhite.net.

Bibliography

Mortimer Adler, How to Speak, How to Listen, (MacMillan) 1983

Roger Ailes with Jon Kraushar, You Are The Message, Secrets of the Master Communicators, (Dow Jones-Irwin) 1988

Roger Axtell, Do's & Taboos Around the World, (Wiley & Sons) 1998

Jason Blume, 6 Steps to Songwriting Success, (Billboard) 1999

Reid Buckley, Strictly Speaking—Reid Buckley's Indispensable Handbook on Public Speaking, (McGraw-Hill, NY) 1999

Julia Cameron & Mark Brown, The Artist's Way, (Putnam) 1992

Judy Carter, Stand-Up Comedy: The Book, (Dell) 1989

Cole & Chinoy, Actors On Acting, (Crown) 1954

Charles W. Eliot, Editor, The Golden Sayings of Epictetus, Harvard Classics, (Collier & Son) 1937

Edward Hegarty, Showmanship in Public Speaking, (McGraw-Hill) 1952

William Henry, III, The Great One—The Life and Legend of Jackie Gleason, (Doubleday) 1992

McBurney & Wrage, The Art of Good Speech, (Prentice-Hall) 1953

Donald S. Passman, All You Need to Know About the Music Business, (Simon & Schuster) 1994

William Safire, Lend Me Your Ears, Great Speeches in History, (W.W. Norton & Co.) 1992

William Safire & Leonard Safire, Good Advice on Writing, (Simon & Schuster) 1992.

Shemel & Krasilovsky, This Business of Music, (Billboard) 1979,

Strunk and White, Elements of Style, (MacMillan) 1959

Granville Toogood, The Articulate Executive, (McGraw-Hill) 1995

T'sai Chih Chung (translated by Brian Bruya), Zen Speaks, Anchor Books, (Doubleday) 1994

Ronald Zalkind, Getting Ahead in the Music Business, (Schirmer) 1979

About Steve Rapson

*"Nobody wishes on their death bed
they had spent more time at the office".*

Or, in Steve's case, any time at the office. After twenty-five years at The Gillette Company, he is now a writer and solo guitarist. Steve's debut CD, *Christmas Guitar*, is sold around the world. He has followed up with four more titles: *Romantic Guitar, Half Irish Guitar, Patriotic Guitar,* and *Original Guitar*, each with a companion book of transcriptions. His two websites are a resource for guitarists and performers.

www.sologuitar.com

www.soloperformer.com.

As a music producer, Steve works with songwriters and performers. His approach to stage work has helped further the careers of many new artists including Kevin So, Mary Gauthier, Ellen Schmidt, British singer/songwriter Paul Chi, and German composer/pianist Ivo Wiesner. He is communications consultant to The American Success Institute in Natick, Massachusetts. *www.success.org.*

The Art of the SoloPerformer is his first book. Steve holds a Masters Degree in Communication Management from Simmons College in Boston. He lives in Quincy, Massachusetts with Rosemary, his wife of thirty years; they married young, it was quite the scandal at the time.